Selected Books and Journals in Science and Engineering

Second Edition

COMPILED BY IRMA JOHNSON

ASSISTED BY OTHER MEMBERS OF THE M.I.T. LIBRARY STAFF.

TECHNOLOGY MONOGRAPHS

Library Series Number One

THE TECHNOLOGY PRESS

Massachusetts Institute of Technology
Cambridge 39, Massachusetts

PREFACE

This list grew out of one originally compiled at the request of the faculty of a new university. Although it reflects this original purpose and some of the subjects emphasized in our own libraries, it is nevertheless hoped that these suggestions may prove useful to any library which must try to cover, in a minimum collection, the various fields of science and engineering.

Intended primarily for undergraduates, the list includes reference works and some treatises and journals for faculty use and for students who anticipate graduate study. We have included, also, some of the bibliographic aids which should prove most useful to a librarian in building a science and engineering collection to meet the specific needs of his own institution.

It will be apparent that many excellent books have had to be omitted. Because brevity was a prime consideration, it was often necessary to choose one or two titles from several works of equal merit. Preference has been given to books in English and out-of-print publications have usually been excluded so that most of the titles suggested might be readily available.

The first edition of this list appeared in 1958. This second edition includes a few corrections and some additions.

December, 1959 Irma Johnson

CONTENTS

I. REFERENCE WORKS

Guides to the literature; Aids to book selection.

American Chemical Society. Literature resources for chemical process industries. (Advances in Chemistry Series, no. 10.) Washington, 1954.

Aslib. British scientific and technical books; a select list of recommended books published in Great Britain and the Commonwealth, 1935-1952. London, James Clarke, 1956.

Aslib. Select list of standard British scientific and technical books. 5th ed. London, Aslib, 1957.

Aslib book-list; a monthly list of recommended scientific and technical books with annotations. 1935. Monthly. London, Aslib.

Columbia University. School of Library Service. Guide to the literature of science... Prepared by Thomas P. Fleming... 2nd ed. New York, Columbia Univ. School of Library Service, 1957.

Crane, E.J. and others. A guide to the literature of chemistry. 2nd ed. New York, Wiley, 1957.

Cumulative book index. 1898. Monthly, with frequent cumulations. New York, Wilson.

Dalton, B.H., ed. Sources of engineering information. Berkeley, Calif., Univ. of California Press, 1948.

Hawkins, R.R., ed. Scientific, medical and technical books: a selected list... 2nd ed. Books published to December 1956. Washington, National Academy of Sciences - National Research Council, 1958. (See also his annual list of outstanding scientific and technical books, published in May issues, Library Journal.)

Holmstrom, J.E. Records and research in engineering and industrial science. 3rd ed. London, Chapman & Hall, 1956.

Howell, J.V. and Levorsen, A.I. Directory of geological material in North America. 2nd ed. Washington, American Geological Institute, 1957.

Jackson, L., ed. Technical libraries: their organization and management. New York, Special Libraries Association, 1951.

Jenkins, F.B. Science reference sources. 2nd ed. Champaign, Ill., Distributed by Illini Union Bookstore, 1958.

London. Science Museum. Library. Books on engineering; a subject catalog of books in the Science Library. London, H.M.S.O., 1957.

Mellon, M.G. Chemical publications; their nature and use. 3rd ed. New York, McGraw-Hill, 1958.

New York Public Library. New technical books; a selected list on industrial arts and engineering added to the New York Public Library. 1915. Bi-monthly. New York, New York Public Library.

Parke, N.G. Guide to the literature of mathematics and physics, including related works on engineering science. 2nd rev. ed. New York, Dover, 1958.

Pearl, R.M. Guide to geologic literature. New York, McGraw-Hill, 1951.

Publishers' trade list annual. Annual. New York, Bowker.

---- Books in print: an author-title series index to the Publishers' trade list annual. Annual. New York, Bowker.

---- Subject guide to Books in print. Annual. New York, Bowker.

Sarton, G. A guide to the history of science; a first guide for the study of the history of science... Waltham, Mass., Chronica Botanica, 1952.

Science reference notes. 1954. Quarterly. New York, Columbia Univ. Science Libraries.

Shank, R., comp. Bibliography of technical reference literature and sources of information. [New York, Columbia Univ.] 1954.

Smith, R.C. Guide to the literature of the zoological sciences. 5th ed. Minneapolis, Minn., Burgess, 1958.

Technical book review index; comp. and ed. in the Technology Dept., Carnegie Library of Pittsburgh. 1935. Monthly, except July and August. New York, Special Libraries Association.

Whitford, R.H. Physics literature; a reference guide. New Brunswick, N.J., Scarecrow Press, 1954.

Winchell, C.M. Guide to reference books. 7th ed. Chicago, American Library Assn., 1951. (Suppl. 1950-52; Second suppl. 1953-55.)

Abstracts and indexes.

Aeronautical engineering index. 1947. Annual. New York, Institute of the Aeronautical Sciences.

Applied science and technology index. 1913. Monthly. New York, H.W. Wilson. (Formerly, Industrial arts index.)

Biological abstracts; from the world's biological research literature. 1926. Monthly. Philadelphia, Pa., Univ. of Pennsylvania.

Chemical abstracts. 1907. Semi-monthly. Washington, American Chemical Society.

Dissertation abstracts; a guide to dissertations and monographs available in microform. 1938. Monthly. Ann Arbor, Mich., University Microfilms.

Engineering index. 1884. Annual (current subscription available also on cards). New York, Engineering Index, Inc.

Geophysical abstracts. 1929. Quarterly, in the Bulletin series of the U.S. Geological Survey. Washington, Gov't. Printing Office.

Mathematical reviews. 1940. Monthly. Providence, R.I., American Mathematical Society.

Nickles, J.M. and others. Bibliography and index of geology exclusive of North America. 1933. Annual. Washington, Geological Society of America.

Nuclear science abstracts. 1948. Semi-monthly. Washington, U.S. Atomic Energy Commission.

Science abstracts: Section A, Physics, Section B, Electrical engineering. 1898. Monthly. London, Institution of Electrical Engineers.

Technical translations. 1959. Semi-monthly. Washington, Gov't. Printing Office.

U.S. government research reports: a monthly listing of government research reports available to industry. 1946. Monthly. Washington, Gov't. Printing Office.

U.S. Geological Survey. Bibliography of North American geology. 1923. Annual, in the Bulletin series of the U.S. Geological Survey. Washington, Gov't. Printing Office.

U.S. Superintendent of Documents. Monthly catalog of United States government publications. 1895. Monthly. Washington, Gov't. Printing Office.

Lists of journals; Union lists.

Association of College and Reference Libraries. Pure and Applied Science Section. A recommended list of basic periodicals in engineering and the engineering sciences. (ACRL monograph no.9) Chicago, Ill., The Association, 1953.

Ayer, firm, Philadelphia. N.W. Ayer & Son's Directory [of] newspapers and periodicals... a guide to publications printed in the United States... 1880. Annual. Philadelphia, Pa., N.W. Ayer & Son, Inc.

British union-catalogue of periodicals; a record of the periodicals of the world, from the seventeenth century to the present day, in British libraries. London, Butterworths Scientific Publs., 1955-58. 4v.

Brown, C.H. Scientific serials; characteristics and lists of most cited publications in mathematics, physics, chemistry, geology, physiology, botany, zoology and entomology. (ACRL monograph no.16.) Chicago, Ill., The Association, 1956.

Canada. National Research Council. Library. Union list of scientific serials in Canadian libraries. Ottawa, National Research Council, 1957.

Chemical abstracts. List of periodicals abstracted by Chemical abstracts, with key to library files and other information. Columbus, Ohio, American Chemical Society, 1956. (Annual supplements.)

Farber, E.I. Classified list of periodicals for the college library. 4th ed., rev. and enl. Boston, Mass., Faxon, 1957.

M.I.T. Library. Current serials and journals in the M.I.T. libraries. Revised to October 1958. Cambridge, Mass., Massachusetts Institute of Technology Libraries, 1959.

New serial titles; a union list of serials commencing publication after December 31, 1949. 1953. Monthly, with annual cumulations which are self-cumulative over five-year periods. Washington, Library of Congress.

Ulrich's periodicals directory; a classified guide to a selected list of current periodicals, foreign and domestic. 8th ed. New York, Bowker, 1956.

Union list of serials in libraries of the United States and Canada. Ed. by Winifred Gregory. 2nd ed. New York, Wilson, 1943. (Suppl. Jan. 1941-Dec. 1943; Second suppl. Jan. 1944-Dec. 1949.)

U.S. Library of Congress. Scientific and technical serial publications, United States, 1950-1953. Washington, Library of Congress, 1954.

World list of scientific periodicals published in the years 1900-1950. 3rd ed. London, Butterworths, 1952. (For additions to this list, see Chemistry and Industry 1953, pp. 1013-14; 1954, pp. 596-97; 1955, pp. 54-57. 1764-67; 1956, pp. 1260-65, etc.)

<u>Handbooks and encyclopedias; Tables; Standards.</u>

American Society for Testing Materials. 1955 book of A.S.T.M. standards, including tentative standards (a triennial publication). Philadelphia, Pa., The Society, 1955-56. 7v. (Suppls. 1956, 1957.)

British Standards Institution. 1958 yearbook. London, British Standards Institution, 1958.

Chemical Rubber Co. Handbook of chemistry and physics; a ready reference book of chemical and physical data. 40th ed. Cleveland, Ohio, Chemical Rubber Publ. Co., 1958.

Encyclopedia Americana; the international reference work. New York and Chicago, Encyclopedia Americana, 1956. 30v.

Eshbach, O.W. Handbook of engineering fundamentals. 2nd ed. New York, Wiley, 1952.

Landolt, H.H. Landolt-Börnstein Zahlenwerte und Funktionen aus Physik, Chemie, Astronomie, Geophysik und Technik. 6th ed. Hrsg. von Arnold Eucken. Berlin, Springer. 1950+. 4v. in many parts (in progress).

Mantell, C.L., ed. Engineering materials handbook. New York, McGraw-Hill, 1958.

National Research Council. International critical tables of numerical data, physics, chemistry and technology. Prepared under the auspices of the International Research Council and the National Academy of Sciences. New York, McGraw-Hill, 1926-33. 7v. and index.

Perry, J. H. and Perry, R. H., eds. Engineering manual. New York, McGraw-Hill, 1959.

Special Libraries Association. Science-Technology Div. Handbook of scientific and technical awards in the United States and Canada, 1900-1952. New York, The Association, 1956.

Van Nostrand's scientific encyclopedia. 3rd ed. Princeton, N.J., Van Nostrand, 1958.

Dictionaries.

Ballentyne, D.W.G. and Walker, L.E.Q. Dictionary of named effects and laws in chemistry, physics and mathematics. London, Chapman & Hall, 1958.

Bray, A., ed. Russian-English technical and scientific dictionary. New York, International Universities Press, 1945.

Callaham, L.I. Russian-English technical and chemical dictionary. New York, Wiley, 1947.

Chamber's technical dictionary; comprising terms used in pure and applied science... Ed. by C.F. Tweney and I.E.C. Hughes. 3rd ed. rev. with suppl. New York, Macmillan, 1958.

Cusset, F. English-French and French-English technical dictionary. 2nd ed. Rev. and enl. New York, Chemical Pub. Co., 1957.

De Vries, L. French-English science dictionary... 2nd ed. New York, McGraw-Hill, 1951.

De Vries, L. German-English science dictionary. 3rd ed. New York, McGraw-Hill, 1959.

De Vries, L. German-English technical and engineering dictionary. New York, McGraw-Hill, 1950.

Flood, W.E. & West, M. Explaining and pronouncing dictionary of scientific and technical words. 2nd ed. London, Longmans, 1955.

Funk and Wagnalls new standard dictionary of the English language. Unabridged ed. New York, Funk and Wagnalls, 1952.

Hyman, C.J., ed. Dictionary of physics and allied sciences. Vol. 1, German-English. New York, Ungar, 1958.

Leibiger, O.W. and Leibiger, I.S. German-English and English-German dictionary for scientists. Ann Arbor, Mich., Edwards, 1950.

Zimmerman, O.T., and Lavine, I. Scientific and technical abbreviations, signs and symbols. 2nd ed. Dover, N.H., Industrial Research Service, 1949.

Directories: Societies; Institutions; Laboratories.

American foundations and their fields. By W.S. Rich. 7th ed. New York, American Foundations Information Service, 1955.

Bates, R.S. Scientific societies in the United States. 2nd ed. New York, Columbia Univ. Press, 1958.

Buttress, F.A. World list of abbreviations of scientific, technological and commercial organizations. London, Leonard Hill, 1954.

Directory of international scientific organizations. 2nd ed. Paris, Unesco, 1953.

Encyclopedia of American associations. 2nd ed. Detroit, Mich., Gale Research Co., 1959.

Index generalis... 1954/55; general yearbook of universities and of higher educational institutions, academies, archives, libraries, scientific institutes... Paris, Dunod, 1955.

Industrial research. 3rd ed. London, Todd Publ. Group, 1956.

Industrial research laboratories of the United States. 10th ed. Washington, National Research Council, 1956.

Minerva; Jahrbuch der gelehrten welt. 34th ed. Berlin, De Gruyter, 1952-56. 2v. in 3.

Scientific and learned societies of Great Britain, a handbook compiled from official sources. 59th ed. London, Allen & Unwin, 1958.

Scientific and technical societies of the United States and Canada. 6th ed. Washington, National Research Council, 1955.

Scientific meetings; a list of forthcoming meetings. 1957. Quarterly. New York, Science-Technology Div., Special Libraries Assn.

Special Libraries Association. Directory of special libraries. Comp. by Isabel L. Towner. New York, The Association, 1953.

U.S. National Science Foundation. Annual report. 1950/51. Annual. Washington, Gov't. Printing Office.

World list of future international meetings. Pt. I. Science, technology, agriculture, medicine. 1959. Monthly. Washington, D.C., Reference Dept., Library of Congress.

World of learning. 9th ed. London, Europa, 1958.

<u>Directories; Biographies: Scientists and engineers.</u>

American men of science; a biographical directory. Ed. by J. Cattell. 9th ed. Vol. 1, Physical sciences; vol. 2, Biological sciences. Lancaster, Pa., Science Press, 1955.

Chemical who's who. 4th ed. New York, Lewis Historical Publ. Co., 1956.

Howard, A.V., ed. Chamber's dictionary of scientists. New York, Dutton, 1951.

International who's who. 1935. Annual. London, Europa.

Leaders in American science. 1958/59. Biennial. Nashville, Tenn., Who's Who in American Education.

Poggendorff, J.C. Biographisch-literarisches handwörterbuch... 1863-1940. 6v. Repr. by Edwards Brothers, Ann Arbor, Mich., 1945. v. 7, 1932-1953. Berlin, Akademie-Verlag, 1955+ (in progress)

Who's who. 1849. Annual. London, Black.

Who's who in America. 1899. Biennial; with monthly suppls. Chicago, Ill., Marquis.

Who's who in British science. London, Leonard Hill, 1953.

Who's who in engineering; a biographical dictionary of the engineering profession. 8th ed. New York, Lewis Historical Publ. Co., 1959.

Aeronautical engineering.

Aircraft yearbook... 1919. Annual. Washington, Aviation Publications.

Baughman, H.E. Aviation dictionary and reference guide. Rev. by E.J. Gentle & C.E. Chapel. 3rd ed. Los Angeles, Calif., Aero Publishers, 1951.

Besserer, C.W. Missile engineering handbook. Princeton, N.J., Van Nostrand, 1958.

Bowman, N.J. Handbook of rockets and guided missiles. Whiting, Ind., Perastadion Press, 1957.

Jane's All the world's aircraft. Comp. and ed. by Leonard Bridgman. 1909. Annual. New York, McGraw-Hill; London, Jane's All the World Aircraft Publishing Co.

Merrill, Grayson and others, eds. Dictionary of guided missiles and space flight. Princeton, N.J., Van Nostrand, 1959.

U.S. Air University. Research Studies Institute. The United States Air Force dictionary. Woodford Agee Heflin, ed. [Maxwell Air Force Base ? Ala.] Air Univ. Press; Washington, Gov't. Printing Office, 1956.

Astronomy.

Bernhard, H.J. and others. New handbook of the heavens. 2nd ed. New York, McGraw-Hill, 1948.

British Astronomical Association. Annual handbook. London, The Association.

Callataÿ, V. de. Atlas of the sky. Transl. and with a preface by Sir H.S. Jones. London, Macmillan, 1958.

Norton, A.P. Star atlas and reference handbook (epoch 1950) for students and amateurs. 10th ed. London, Gall and Inglis, 1946.

U.S. Nautical Almanac Office. American ephemeris and nautical almanac. 1852. Annual. Washington, Gov't. Printing Office. (Now the same as Great Britain. Nautical Almanac Office. The astronomical ephemeris.)

Biology.

Bailey, L.H. and others. Manual of cultivated plants most commonly grown in the continental United States and Canada. Rev. ed. New York, Macmillan, 1949.

Cambridge natural history. Ed. by Sir S.F. Harmer and Sir A.E. Shipley. Repr. ed. Weinheim, Germany, Engelmann, 1958+ (c1895-1909). 10v. (in progress)

Cowdry, E.V. Laboratory technique in biology and medicine. 3rd ed. Baltimore, Md., Williams & Wilkins, 1952.

Dorland, W.A.N. Illustrated medical dictionary. 23rd ed. Ed. by L.B. Arey and others. Philadelphia, Pa., Saunders, 1957.

Fisher, R.A. and Yates, F. Statistical tables for biological, agricultural and medical research. 5th ed., rev. and enl. Edinburgh, Oliver and Boyd, 1957.

Glasser, O. Medical physics. Chicago, Ill., Yearbook Publishers, 1944-50. 2v.

Gleason, H.A. The new Britton and Brown illustrated flora of the Northeastern United States and adjacent Canada. New York, New York Botanical Garden, 1952. 3v.

Gray, A. Manual of botany; a handbook of the flowering plants and ferns of the Central and Northeastern United States and adjacent Canada. 8th ed... by Merritt Lyndon Fernald. New York, American Book, 1950.

Henderson, I.F. and Henderson, W.D. Dictionary of scientific terms... in biology, botany, zoology, anatomy, cytology, genetics, embryology, physiology. 6th ed. Ed. by J.H. Kenneth. Edinburgh, Oliver and Boyd, 1957.

Jackson, B.D. Glossary of botanic terms. 4th ed. New York, Hafner, 1949.

Jaeger, E.C. A source-book of biological names and terms. 2nd ed. Springfield, Ill., C.C. Thomas, 1950.

Lee, A.B. The microtomist's vade-mecum; a handbook of the methods of animal and plant microscopic technique. Ed. by J. Brontë Gatenby and H.W. Beams. 11th ed. London, J. & A. Churchill, 1950.

Palmer, E.L. Fieldbook of natural history. New York, McGraw-Hill, 1949.

Spector, W. Handbook of biological data. Philadelphia, Pa., Saunders, 1956.

Chemical engineering.

Encyclopedia of chemical technology. Ed. by R.E. Kirk and others. New York, Interscience Encyclopedias, 1947-56. 15v. (Suppl. 1 [1957])

Faith, W.L. and others. Industrial chemicals. 2nd ed. New York, Wiley, 1957.

Hopkins, A.A., ed. Standard American encyclopedia of formulas. New York, Grosset & Dunlap, 1953.

Lange, N.A., comp. Handbook of chemistry; a reference volume... to chemical and physical data used in laboratory work and manufacturing. 9th ed. Sandusky, Ohio, Handbook Publishers, 1956.

Perry, J.H. Chemical engineers' handbook. 3rd ed. New York, McGraw-Hill, 1950.

Thorpe, J.F. Thorpe's dictionary of applied chemistry. 4th ed. London, Longmans, 1937-55. 12v.

Ullmann, F. Encyklopädie der technischen Chemie. 3rd ed. Ed. by W. Foerst. München-Berlin, Urban and Schwarzenberg, 1951+. v. 1+(in progress)

Chemistry.

Association of Official Agricultural Chemists. Official methods of analysis. 8th ed. Washington, The Association, 1955.

Beilstein, F.K. Handbuch der organischen chemie. 4. Aufl. Berlin, Springer, 1918-44. 64v. in 53.

Clark, G.L. Encyclopedia of chemistry. New York, Reinhold, 1957. (Suppl. 1958)

Condensed Chemical dictionary. 5th ed. New York, Reinhold, 1956.

Heilbron, Sir I. and Bunbury, H.M., eds. Dictionary of organic compounds, the constitution and physical and chemical properties of the principal carbon compounds and their derivatives... New rev. ed. New York, Oxford Univ. Press, 1953. 4v.

Huntress, E.H. A brief introduction to the use of Beilstein's Handbuch der organischen chemie. 2nd ed. New York, Wiley, 1938.

Inorganic syntheses. New York, McGraw-Hill, 1939-57. 5v.

Jacobson, C.A. and Hampel, C., eds. Encyclopedia of chemical reactions. New York, Reinhold. 1946-59. 8v.

Mellor, J.W. Comprehensive treatise on inorganic and theoretical chemistry. London, Longmans, Green, 1922-37. 16v. (Suppl. 2, Pts. 1-2, 1956-59; others projected.)

Merck index of chemicals and drugs; an encyclopedia for the chemist, pharmacist, physician and allied professions. 6th ed. Rahway, N.J., Merck Co., 1952.

Organic reactions. New York, Wiley, 1942-57. 9v.

Organic syntheses; an annual publication of satisfactory methods for the preparation of organic chemicals. 1921. Annual. New York, Wiley.

Rodd, E.H., ed. Chemistry of carbon compounds, a modern comprehensive treatise. New York, Amsterdam, Elsevier, 1951+. 5v. (projected) in 8 ? parts.

Scott, W.W. Standard methods of chemical analysis. 5th ed. New York, Van Nostrand, 1939. 2v.

Van Nostrand chemist's dictionary. Princeton, N.J., Van Nostrand, 1953.

Civil and sanitary engineering; Building construction.

Abbett, R.W., ed. American civil engineering practice. New York, Wiley, 1956-57. 3v.

American Institute of Steel Construction. Steel construction; a manual for architects, engineers, and fabricators of buildings and other steel structures. 5th ed. New York, The Institute, 1947.

Creager, W.P. and Justin, J.D. Hydroelectric handbook. 2nd ed. New York, Wiley, 1950.

Davis, C.V., ed. Handbook of applied hydraulics. 2nd ed. New York, McGraw-Hill, 1952.

Hansen, H.J., ed. Timber engineers' handbook. New York, Wiley, 1948.

Hool, G.A. and Johnson, N.C. Concrete engineers' handbook; data for the design and construction of plain and reinforced concrete structures. 2nd ed. New York, McGraw-Hill. (in press)

Ketchum, M.S. Structural engineers' handbook; data for the design and construction of steel bridges and buildings. 3rd ed. New York, McGraw-Hill, 1924.

King, H.W. Handbook of hydraulics for the solution of hydraulic problems. 4th ed. New York, McGraw-Hill, 1954.

Merritt, F.S., ed. Building construction handbook. New York, McGraw-Hill, 1958.

Probst, E.H. and Comrie, J., eds. Civil engineering reference book. London, Butterworths Scientific Publs., 1951.

Ramsey, C.G. Architectural graphic standards for architects, engineers, decorators, builders and draftsmen. 5th ed. New York, Wiley, 1956.

Seelye, E.E. Data book for civil engineers. New York, Wiley, 1951. 3v.

Timber Engineering Company. Timber design and construction handbook. New York, F.W. Dodge Corp., 1956.

Trautwine, J.C. Civil engineers reference book. 21st ed. Ithaca, New York, Cornell Univ. Press, 1937.

U.S. Forest Products Laboratory, Madison, Wisconsin. Wood handbook: basic information on wood as a material of construction with data for its use in design and specification. Washington, Gov't. Printing Office, 1955.

U.S. Bureau of Reclamation. Concrete manual; a manual for the control of concrete construction. 6th ed. Denver, Colo. [Gov't. Printing Office] 1955.

Urquhart, L.C. Civil engineering handbook. 4th ed. New York, McGraw-Hill, 1959.

Electrical engineering.

American Radio Relay League. Radio amateur's handbook, a manual of amateur high frequency radio communication. Annual. Hartford, Conn., American Radio Relay League.

Henney, Keith, ed. Radio engineering handbook. 5th ed. New York, McGraw-Hill, 1959.

Hunter, L.P., ed. Handbook of semiconductor electronics; a practical manual covering the physics, technology and circuit applications of transistors, diodes and photocells. New York, McGraw-Hill, 1956.

International Telephone and Telegraph Corporation. Reference data for radio engineers. 4th ed. New York, The Corporation, 1956.

Knowlton, A.E., ed. Standard handbook for electrical engineers. 9th ed. New York, McGraw-Hill, 1957.

Pender, H. and others, eds. Electrical engineers' handbook. 4th ed. New York, McGraw-Hill, 1957.

Sarbacher, R. I. Encyclopedic dictionary of electronics and nuclear engineering. Englewood Cliffs, N. J., Prentice-Hall, 1959.

Truxal, J.G., ed. Control engineer's handbook; servomechanisms, regulators and automatic feedback control systems. New York, McGraw-Hill, 1958.

<u>Geology and geophysics.</u>

American Geological Institute. A glossary of geology and related sciences. Washington, The Institute, 1957.

American Meteorological Society. Meteorological glossary. Boston, Mass., The Society, 1957.

Berry, F.A. and others, eds. Handbook of meteorology. New York, McGraw-Hill, 1945.

Chambers's mineralogical dictionary. New ed. New York, Chemical Publ. Co., 1948.

Dana, E.S. and Hurlbut, C.S. The system of mineralogy. 7th ed. New York, Wiley, 1944-51. 2v.

Hey, M.H. An index of mineral species and varieties. 2nd ed., rev. London, British Museum, 1955.

Lahee, F.H. Field geology. 5th ed. New York, McGraw-Hill, 1952.

National Research Council. Handbook of physical constants. (Geol. Soc. of America, Spec. Paper no. 36.) New York, Geological Society of America, 1942.

Smithsonian meterological tables. 6th ed. Washington, Smithsonian Institution, 1951.

U.S. Dept. of Agriculture. Climate and man, yearbook of agriculture, 1941. Washington, Gov't. Printing Office, 1941.

U.S. Bureau of Mines. Minerals yearbook, 1957. Washington, Gov't. Printing Office, 1958-59.

Mathematics.

Burington, R.S. Handbook of mathematical tables and formulas. 3rd ed. Sandusky, Ohio, Handbook Publishers, 1948.

Burington, R.S. and May, D.C. Handbook of probability and statistics with tables. Sandusky, Ohio, Handbook Publishers, 1953.

Comrie, L.J., ed. Barlow's tables of squares, square roots, cube roots and reciprocals of all integers up to 12,500. 4th ed. New York, Chemical Publishing Co., 1952.

Comrie, L.J. Chamber's six-figure mathematical tables. Edinburgh, W. & R. Chambers, 1948-49. 2v.

Dwight, H.B. Mathematical tables of elementary and some higher mathematical functions. 2nd ed. New York, Dover, 1958.

Dwight, H.B. Tables of integrals and other mathematical data. 3rd ed. New York, Macmillan, 1957.

Gröbner, W. and Hofreiter, N., eds. Integraltafel. Wien, Springer, 1957, 1950. 2v. (v. 1, 2nd ed.)

Jahnke, E. and Emde, F. Tables of functions with formulae and curves. (Funktionentafeln mit Formeln und Kurven). 4th ed. New York, Dover, 1945.

James, G. and James, R.C., eds. Mathematics dictionary. Multilingual ed. Princeton, N.J., Van Nostrand, 1959.

Peirce, B.O. A short table of integrals. 4th ed. Rev. by Ronald M. Foster. Boston, Mass., Ginn, 1956.

Peters, J. Seven-place values of trigonometric functions. New York, Van Nostrand, 1942.

Schütte, K., ed. Index mathematischer Tafelwerke und Tabellen aus allen gebieten der Naturwissenschaften. Munchen, R. Oldenbourg, 1955. (Text in German and English.)

Spenceley, G.W. and others. Smithsonian logarithmic tables to base e and base 10. Washington, Smithsonian Institution, 1952.

Vega, G. Seven place logarithmic tables of numbers and trigonometric functions. New York, Hafner, 1957.

Mechanical engineering.

American Society of Heating and Air Conditioning Engineers. Heating, ventilating, air conditioning guide. Annual. New York, The Society.

American Society of Mechanical Engineers. ASME handbook. New York, McGraw-Hill, 1953-58. 4v.

American Society of Refrigerating Engineers. Air conditioning, refrigerating data book. New York, The Society, 1955. 2v. (v. 1, 9th ed.; v. 2, 5th ed.)

Diesel engineering handbook. 9th ed. New York, Diesel Publications, 1955.

Hetenyi, M., ed. Handbook of experimental stress analysis. New York, Wiley, 1950.

Johnson, A.J. and Auth, G.H. Fuels and combustion handbook. New York, McGraw-Hill, 1951.

Keenan, J.H. and Kaye, J. Gas tables; thermodynamic properties of air, products of combustion and component gases, compressible flow functions including those of Ascher H. Shapiro and Gilbert M. Edelman. New York, Wiley, 1948.

Keenan, J.H. and Kaye, J. Thermodynamic properties of air, including polytropic functions. New York, Wiley, 1945.

Keenan, J.H. and Keyes, F.G. Thermodynamic properties of steam, including data for the liquid and solid phases. New York, Wiley, 1936.

Kent, W. Mechanical engineers' handbook. 12th ed. New York, Wiley, 1950. 2v.

Machinery's handbook; a reference book for the mechanical engineer. . . and machinist. . . 16th ed. New York, Industrial Press, 1959.

Marks, L.S. Mechanical engineers' handbook. 6th ed., edited by T. Bauermeister. New York, McGraw-Hill, 1958.

Miner, D.F. and Seastone, J.B., eds. Handbook of engineering materials. New York, Wiley, 1955.

Society of Automotive Engineers. 1957 SAE handbook. New York, The Society, 1957.

Mining and metallurgy.

American Foundrymen's Society. Cast metals handbook. 4th ed. Des Plaines, Ill., 1957.

American Society for Metals. Metals handbook. Cleveland, Ohio, The Society. 1948. (2 suppls., 1954-55)

American Welding Society. Welding handbook. 3rd ed. New York, The Society, 1950.

Hampel, C.A., ed. Rare metals handbook. New York, Reinhold, 1954.

Merriman, A.D. Dictionary of metallurgy. London, Pitman, 1958.

Osborne, A.K., comp. An encyclopedia of the iron and steel industry. New York, Philosophical Library, 1956.

Pearson, W.B. Handbook of lattice spacings and structures of metals and alloys. New York, Pergamon Press, 1958.

Peele, R. and Church, J.A., eds. Mining engineers' handbook. 3rd ed. New York, Wiley, 1941. 2v.

Smithells, C.J., ed. Metals reference book. 2nd ed. New York, Interscience, 1955.

Uhlig, H.H., ed. The corrosion handbook. New York, Wiley, 1948.

Nuclear engineering.

Etherington, H., ed. Nuclear engineering handbook. New York, McGraw-Hill, 1958.

Physics.

American Institute of Physics. Physics handbook. New York, McGraw-Hill, 1957.

Condon, E.U. and Odishaw, H. Handbook of physics. New York, McGraw-Hill, 1958.

Forsythe, W.E. Smithsonian physical tables. 9th rev. ed. Washington, Smithsonian Institution, 1954.

Frisch, O.R., ed. The nuclear handbook. London, G. Newnes, 1958.

Glazebrook, Sir R.T., ed. A dictionary of applied physics. Reprint ed. Gloucester, Mass., Peter Smith, 1950(c1922-23). 5v.

Gray, H.J., ed. Dictionary of physics. London, Longmans, Green, 1958.

Handbuch der physik (Encyclopedia of physics). Ed. by S. Flügge. Berlin, Springer, 1956+. v. 1+(in progress)

International dictionary of physics and electronics. Princeton, N.J., Van Nostrand, 1956.

Kaye, G.W.C. and Laby, T.H. Tables of physical and chemical constants. 11th ed. London, Longmans, Green, 1955.

Maerz, A.J. and Paul, M.R. Dictionary of color. 2nd ed. New York, McGraw-Hill, 1950.

Menzel, D.H. Fundamental formulas of physics. New York, Prentice-Hall, 1955.

National Research Council. Conference on Glossary of Terms in Nuclear Science and Technology. A glossary of terms in nuclear science and technology. New York, American Society of Mechanical Engineers, 1957.

<u>History of science and technology.</u>

Sarton, G. Introduction to the history of science. Baltimore, Md. Published for Carnegie Institution of Washington by the Williams and Wilkins Co., 1927-48. 3v. in 5.

Singer, C.J. and others, eds. A history of technology. Oxford, Clarendon Press, 1954-58. 5v.

II. TEXTBOOKS AND TREATISES

Aeronautical engineering.

Aerodynamic theory; a general review of progress. W.F. Durand, editor-in-chief. Berlin, Springer, 1935. 6v. (Repr. by Durand Reprinting Committee, California Institute of Technology, Pasadena, 1943.)

Bisplinghoff, R.L. and others. Aeroelasticity. Reading, Mass., Addison-Wesley, 1955.

Bonney, E.A. and others. Aerodynamics, propulsion, structures and design practice. Princeton, N.J., Van Nostrand, 1956.

Bussard, R.W. and De Lauer, R.D. Nuclear rocket propulsion. New York, McGraw-Hill, 1958.

Corning, Gerald. Airplane design. College Park, Md. [The Author] 1954. (Lithoprinted by Edwards Bros., Ann Arbor, Mich.)

Dommasch, D.O. and others. Airplane aerodynamics. 2nd ed. New York, Pitman, 1957.

Donovan, A.F. and Lawrence, H.R., eds. Aerodynamic components of aircraft at high speeds. Princeton, N.J., Princeton Univ. Press, 1957.

Donovan, A.F. and others, eds. High speed problems of aircraft and experimental methods. Princeton, N.J. Princeton Univ. Press. (In prep.)

Draper, C.S. and others. Intrument engineering. New York, McGraw-Hill, 1952+. 3v. in 4 (projected).

Ehricke, K.A. Space flight. Princeton, N.J., Van Nostrand. (In prgs.)

Emmons, H.W., ed. Fundamentals of gas dynamics. Princeton, N.J., Princeton Univ. Press, 1958.

Etkin, Bernard. Dynamics of flight; stability and control. New York, Wiley, 1959.

Gessow, Alfred and Myers, G.C., Jr. Aerodynamics of the helicopter. New York, Macmillan, 1952.

Great Britain. Aeronautical Research Comm. Fluid Motion Panel. Modern developments in fluid dynamics... Ed. by S. Goldstein. Oxford, Clarendon Press, 1938. 2v.

Hawthorne, W.R., ed. Aerodynamics of turbines and compressors. Princeton, N.J., Princeton Univ. Press. (In prep.)

Hawthorne, W.R., ed. Design and performance of gas turbine power plants. Princeton, N.J., Princeton Univ. Press. (In prep.)

Jerger, J.J. and Freitag, R.F. Systems engineering; range testing. Princeton, N.J., Van Nostrand. (In prep.)

Kuethe, A.M. and Schetzer, J.D. Foundations of aerodynamics. 2nd ed. New York, Wiley, 1959. (projected)

Ladenburg, R.W. and others, eds. Physical measurements in gas dynamics and combustion. Princeton, N.J., Princeton Univ. Press, 1954.

Lancaster, O.E., ed. Jet propulsion engines. Princeton, N.J., Princeton Univ. Press, 1959.

Lees, L. and Lin, C.C., eds. Laminar flows and transition to turbulence. Princeton, N.J., Princeton Univ. Press. (In prep.)

Lees, L. and Lin, C.C., eds. Turbulent flows and heat transfer. Princeton, N.J., Princeton Univ. Press. (In prep.)

Liepmann, H.W. and Roshko, A. Elements of gasdynamics. New York, Wiley [c1957].

Locke, A.S. Guidance. Princeton, N.J., Van Nostrand, 1955.

Merrill, G.H. and others. Operations research, armament, launching. Princeton, N.J., Van Nostrand, 1956.

Niles, A.S. and Newell, J.S. Airplane structures. New York, Wiley, 1954, 1943. 2v. (v. 1, 4th ed.; v. 2, 3rd ed.)

Northrop Aeronautical Institute. Aircraft basic science. Rev. ed. New York, McGraw-Hill, 1953.

Northrop Aeronautical Institute. Aircraft power plants. Rev. ed. New York, McGraw-Hill, 1955.

Peery, D.J. Aircraft structures. New York, McGraw-Hill, 1950.

Perkins, C.D. and Hage, R.E. Airplane performance stability and control. New York, Wiley, 1949.

Rauscher, Manfred. Introduction to aeronautical dynamics. New York, Wiley, 1953.

Sears, W.R., ed. General theory of high speed aerodynamics. Princeton, N.J., Princeton Univ. Press, 1954.

Sutton, G.P. Rocket propulsion elements; an introduction to the engineering of rockets. 2nd ed. New York, Wiley, 1956.

Wood, K.D. Technical aerodynamics. 3rd ed. Ann Arbor, Mich., Ulrich's Book Store, Published by the author [1955].

Zuerow, M.J. Aircraft and missile propulsion. New York, Wiley, 1958. 2v.

Astronomy.

Abetti, G. The sun. Transl. by J.B. Sidgwick. New York, Macmillan, 1957.

Aller, L.H. Astrophysics; the atmospheres of the sun and stars. New York, Ronald Press, 1953.

Baker, R.H. Astronomy, a textbook for university and college students. 7th ed. Princeton, N.J., Van Nostrand, 1959.

Freundlich, E.F. Celestial mechanics. New York, Pergamon Press, 1958.

Gaposchkin, C.H. Introduction to astronomy. New York, Prentice-Hall, 1955.

Hynek, J.A., ed. Astrophysics: a topical symposium. New York, McGraw-Hill, 1951.

Russell, H.N. and others. Astronomy; a revision of Young's Manual of astronomy. Boston, Mass., Ginn, 1945, 1938. 2v. (v. 1 is Rev. ed.)

Shapley, H. and Howarth, H.E. A source book in astronomy. Cambridge, Mass., Harvard Univ. Press, 1956.

Sidgwick, J.B. Amateur astronomer's handbook. New York, Macmillan, 1955.

Sidgwick, J.B. Observational astronomy for amateurs. London, Faber and Faber, 1955.

Whipple, F.L. Earth, moon and planets. Cambridge, Mass., Harvard Univ. Press, 1941.

Biology.

Allee, W.C. and others. Principles of animal ecology. Philadelphia, Pa., Saunders, 1949.

Arey, L.B. Developmental anatomy; a textbook and laboratory manual of embryology. 6th ed. Philadelphia, Pa., Saunders, 1954.

Baldwin, E. Dynamic aspects of biochemistry. 3rd ed. Cambridge [Eng.] University Press, 1957.

Baldwin, E. An introduction to comparative biochemistry. 3rd ed. Cambridge [Eng.] University Press, 1948.

Benson, L. Elements of plant classification. Boston, Mass., D.C. Heath, 1956.

Bonner, J. and Galston, A.W. Principles of plant physiology. San Francisco, Calif., W.H. Freeman, 1952.

Carlson, A.J. and Johnson, V.E. The machinery of the body. 4th ed. Chicago, Ill., Univ. of Chicago Press, 1953.

Darwin, C. Origin of species and descent of man. New York, Modern Library, n.d.

Davson, H. Textbook of general physiology. London, J. & A. Churchill, 1951.

De Robertis, E.D.P. and others. General cytology. 2nd ed. Philadelphia, Pa., Saunders, 1954.

Dobzhansky, T. Genetics and the origin of species. 3rd ed. New York, Columbia Univ. Press, 1951.

Esau, K. Plant anatomy. New York, Wiley, 1953.

Frobisher, M. Fundamentals of microbiology. 6th ed. Philadelphia, Pa., Saunders, 1957.

textbooks and treatises

Fruton, J.S. and Simmonds, S. General biochemistry. 2nd ed. New York, Wiley, 1958.

Fuller, H.J. The plant world; a text in college botany. 3rd ed. New York, Holt, 1955.

Fulton, J.F., ed. A textbook of physiology. 17th ed. Philadelphia, Pa., Saunders, 1956.

Gabriel, M.L. and Fogel, S. Great experiments in biology. Englewood Cliffs, N.J., Prentice-Hall, 1955.

Gage, S.H. The microscope. 17th ed. Ithaca, New York, Comstock, 1941.

Gregory, W.K. Evolution emerging; a survey of changing patterns from primeval life to man. New York, Macmillan, 1951. 2v.

Hawk, P.B. and others. Practical physiological chemistry. 13th ed. New York, Blakiston [1954].

Huxley, J. Evolution; the modern synthesis. New York, Harper, 1942.

Hyman, L.H. The invertebrates. New York, McGraw-Hill, 1940-59. 5v.

Lawrence, G.H.M. Taxonomy of vascular plants. New York, Macmillan, 1951.

Maximov, H.H. and Bloom, W. Textbook of histology. 7th ed. Philadelphia, Pa., Saunders, 1957.

Mayr, E. and others. Methods and principles of systematic zoology. New York, McGraw-Hill, 1953.

Odum, E.P. Fundamentals of ecology. Philadelphia, Pa., Saunders, 1953.

Oparin, A.I. The origin of life on the earth. 3rd ed. Transl. from the Russian by A. Synge. Edinburgh, Oliver & Boyd, 1957.

Oster, G. and Pollister, A.W., eds. Physical techniques in biological research. New York, Academic Press, 1955-56. 3 v.

Parker, T.J. and Haswell, W.A. Textbook of zoology. 6th ed. Vol. 1 rev. by Otto Lowenstein; vol. 2 rev. by C. Forster-Cooper. London, Macmillan, 1951. 2v.

Romer, A.S. The vertebrate body. 2nd ed. Philadelphia, Pa., Saunders, 1955.

Romer, A.S. The vertebrate story. 4th ed. Chicago, Ill., Univ. of Chicago Press, 1959.

Simpson, G.G. and others. Life; an introduction to college biology. New York, Harcourt, Brace, 1957.

Srb, A.K. and Owen, R.D. General genetics. San Francisco, Calif., Freeman, 1952.

Stacy, R.W. and others. Essentials of biological and medical physics. New York, McGraw-Hill, 1955.

Storer, T.I. and Usinger, R.L. General zoology. 3rd ed. New York, McGraw-Hill, 1957.

Villee, C.A. Biology. 3rd ed. Philadelphia, Pa., Saunders, 1957.

Waddington, C.H. Principles of embryology. London, George Allen & Unwin, 1956.

Weaver, J.E. and Clements, F.E. Plant ecology. 2nd ed. New York, McGraw-Hill, 1938.

Wilson, C.L. Botany. New York, Dryden, 1952.

Young, J.Z. The life of mammals. Oxford, Clarendon Press, 1957.

Young, J.Z. The life of vertebrates. London, Oxford Univ. Press, 1950.

Chemical engineering.

Badger, W.L. and Banchero, J.T. Introduction to chemical engineering. New York, McGraw-Hill, 1955.

Brown, G.G. and others. Unit operations. New York, Wiley, 1950.

Coulson, J.M. and Richardson, J.F. Chemical engineering. London, Pergamon Press, 1954. 2v.

Cremer, H.W., ed. Chemical engineering practice. London, Butterworth, 1956+. 12v. (projected)

Hougen, O.A. and others. Chemical process principles. 2nd ed. New York, Wiley, 1954+. 3v. (projected)

Jordan, D.C. Chemical pilot plant practice. New York, Interscience, 1955.

Lewis, W.K., Squires, L., and Broughton, G. Industrial chemistry of colloidal and amorphous materials. New York, Macmillan, 1954.

Lewis, W.K. and others. Industrial stoichiometry. New York, McGraw-Hill, 1954.

McAdams, W.H. Heat transmission. 3rd ed. New York, McGraw-Hill, 1954.

McCabe, W.L. and Smith, J. Unit operations of chemical engineering. New York, McGraw-Hill, 1956.

Read, W.T. Industrial chemistry. 3rd ed. New York, Wiley, 1943.

Riegel, R. Chemical process machinery. 2nd ed. New York, Reinhold, 1953.

Robinson, C.S. and Gilliland, E.R. Elements of fractional distillation. 4th ed. New York, McGraw-Hill, 1950.

Rogers, A. Industrial chemistry; a manual for the student and manufacturer. 6th ed. by C.C. Furnas. Princeton, N.J., Van Nostrand, 1942. 2v.

Sherwood, T.K. and Pigford, R.L. Absorption and extraction. 2nd ed. New York, McGraw-Hill, 1952.

Shreve, R.N. The chemical process industries. New York, McGraw-Hill, 1956.

Smith, M.L. and Stinson, K.W. Fuels and combustion. New York, McGraw-Hill, 1952.

Vilbrandt, F.C. Chemical engineering plant design. 3rd ed. New York, McGraw-Hill, 1949.

Walker, W.H. and others. Principles of chemical engineering. 3rd ed. New York, McGraw-Hill, 1937.

Weber, H.C. and Meissner, H.P. Thermodynamics for chemical engineers. 2nd ed. New York, Wiley, 1957.

Chemistry.

Benson, S.W. Chemical calculations; an introduction to the use of mathematics in chemistry. New York, Wiley, 1952.

Buerger, M.J. Elementary crystallography; an introduction to the fundamental geometrical features of crystals. New York, Wiley, 1956.

Daniels, F. and Alberty, R.A. Physical chemistry. New York, Wiley, 1955.

Denbiegh, K. Principles of chemical equilibrium. Cambridge [Eng.] University Press, 1955.

Dodd, R.E. and Robinson, P.L. Experimental inorganic chemistry. Amsterdam, Houston, Elsevier, 1954.

Eyring, H. and others. Quantum chemistry. New York, Wiley, 1944.

Farber, E. The evolution of chemistry; a history of its ideas, methods, materials. New York, Ronald, 1952.

Fieser, L.F. and Fieser, M. Organic chemistry. 3rd ed. New York, Reinhold, 1956.

Friedlander, G. and Kennedy, J. Nuclear and radiochemistry. New York, Wiley, 1955.

Fritz, J.S. and Hammond, G.S. Quantitative organic analysis. New York, Wiley, 1957.

Gilman, H., ed. Organic chemistry; an advanced treatise. New York, Wiley, 1943-53. 4v. (v. 1-2, 2nd ed.)

Gould, E.S. Inorganic reactions and structure. New York, Holt, 1955.

Hamilton, L.F. and Simpson, S.G. Calculations of analytical chemistry. 5th ed. New York, McGraw-Hill, 1954.

Hamilton, L.F. and Simpson, S.G. Quantitative chemical analysis. 10th ed. New York, Macmillan, 1952.

Hildebrand, J.H. and Powell, R.E. Principles of chemistry. 6th ed. New York, Macmillan, 1952.

Hine, J. Physical organic chemistry. New York, McGraw-Hill, 1956.

Kennard, E.H. Kinetic theory of gases. New York, McGraw-Hill, 1938.

Latimer, W.M. and Hildebrand, J.H. Reference book of inorganic chemistry. 3rd ed. New York, Macmillan, 1951.

Lederer, E. and Lederer, M. Chromatography; a review of principles and applications. 2nd ed. Amsterdam, Elsevier, 1957.

Leicester, H.M. and Klickstein, H.S. Source book in chemistry, 1400-1900. Cambridge, Mass., Harvard Univ. Press, 1956.

Moeller, T. Inorganic chemistry. New York, Wiley, 1952.

Moore, W.J. Physical chemistry. 2nd ed. Englewood Cliffs, N.J., Prentice-Hall, 1955.

Noller, C.R. Chemistry of organic compounds. 2nd ed. Philadelphia, Pa., Saunders, 1957.

Noyes, A.A. and Swift, E.H. A course of instruction in the qualitative chemical analysis of inorganic substance. 10th ed. New York, Macmillan, 1942.

Noyes, A.A. and Sherrill, M.S. A course of study in chemical principles. 2nd ed. New York, Macmillan [1938].

Partington, J.R. Advanced treatise on physical chemistry. London, Longmans, 1949-54. 4v.

Partington, J.R. A textbook of inorganic chemistry. 6th ed. London, Macmillan, 1950.

Pauling, L.C. Nature of the chemical bond and the structure of molecules and crystals; an introduction to modern structural chemistry. 2nd ed. Ithaca, N.Y., Cornell Univ. Press, 1940.

Pitzer, K.S. Quantum chemistry. New York, Prentice-Hall, 1953.

Robertson, G.R. Laboratory practice of organic chemistry. 3rd ed. New York, Macmillan, 1954.

Royals, E.E. Advanced organic chemistry. Englewood Cliffs, N.J., Prentice-Hall, 1954.

Shriner, R.L. and others. Systematic identification of organic compounds: a laboratory manual. 4th ed. London, Chapman & Hall, 1956.

Sidgwick, N.V. Chemical elements and their compounds. New York, Oxford Univ. Press, 1950. 2v.

Slater, J.C. Introduction to chemical physics. New York, McGraw-Hill, 1939.

Steiner, L.E. and Campbell, J.A. General chemistry. New York, Macmillan, 1955.

Taylor, H.S. and Glasstone, S. Treatise on physical chemistry. 3rd ed. Princeton, N.J., Van Nostrand, 1942+. 5v. (projected)

Wagner, R.B. and Zook, H.D. Synthetic organic chemistry. New York, Wiley, 1953.

Weeks, M. E. Discovery of the elements. 6th ed. Easton, Pa., Journal of Chemical Education, 1956.

Weissberger, A. Technique of organic chemistry. 2nd ed. New York, Interscience, 1949. 7v.

Wells, A.F. Structural inorganic chemistry. 2nd ed. Oxford, Clarendon, 1950.

Wheland, G.W. Resonance in organic chemistry. New York, Wiley, 1955.

Willard, H.H. and others. Instrumental methods of analysis. 3rd ed. Princeton, N.J., Van Nostrand, 1958.

Civil and sanitary engineering; Building construction.

American Society of Civil Engineers. Committee on Hydrology. Hydrology handbook; adopted Jan. 17, 1949. New York, The Society, 1957.

Babbitt, H.E. Engineering in public health. New York, McGraw-Hill, 1952.

Babbitt, H.E. Sewerage and sewage treatment. 8th ed. New York, Wiley, 1958.

Babbitt, H.E. and Doland, J.J. Water supply engineering. 5th ed. New York, McGraw-Hill, 1955.

Barrows, H.K. Water power engineering. 3rd ed. New York, McGraw-Hill, 1943.

textbooks and treatises

Bateman, J.H. Introduction to highway engineering. 5th ed. New York, Wiley, 1948.

Breed, C.B. and Hosmer, G.L. Principles and practice of surveying. 9th ed. New York, Wiley, 1959, 1953. 2v. (Vol. 2 is 7th ed.)

Conference on Biological Waste Treatment, Manhattan College, April 13-15, 1955. Biological treatment of sewage and industrial wastes; papers presented at the conference. v. 1, Aerobic oxidation. New York, Reinhold, 1956.

Creager, W.P. and others. Engineering for dams. New York, Wiley, 1945. 3v.

Dietz, A.G.H. Materials of construction: wood, plastics, fabrics. Princeton, N.J., Van Nostrand, 1949.

Dunham, C.W. Foundations of structures. New York, McGraw-Hill, 1950.

Dunham, C.W. The theory and practice of reinforced concrete. 3rd ed. New York, McGraw-Hill, 1953.

Ehlers, V.M. and Steel, E.W. Municipal and rural sanitation. 4th ed. New York, McGraw-Hill, 1950.

Fair, G.M. and Geyer, J.C. Water supply and waste water disposal. New York, Wiley, 1954.

Frevert, R.K. and others. Soil and water conservation engineering. New York, Wiley, 1955.

Gay, C.M. and others. Materials and methods of architectural construction. 3rd ed. New York, Wiley, 1958.

Great Britain. Road Research Laboratory. Soil mechanics for road engineers. London, H.M.S.O., 1952.

Hardenbergh, W.A. Water supply and purification. 3rd ed. Scranton, Pa., International Textbook, 1952.

Hay, W.W. Railroad engineering. New York, Wiley, 1953-54. 2v.

Hennes, R.G. and Ekse, M.I. Fundamentals of transportation engineering. New York, McGraw-Hill, 1955.

Hewes, L.L. and Oglesby, C.H. Highway engineering. New York, Wiley, 1954.

Hool, G.A. and Kinne, W.S., eds. Foundations, abutments and footings. Rev. by R.R. Zipprodt and E.J. Kilcawley. 2nd ed. New York, McGraw-Hill, 1943.

Huntington, W.C. Building construction. 2nd ed. New York, Wiley, 1941.

Imhoff, K. and Fair, G.M. Sewage treatment. 2nd ed. New York, Wiley, 1956.

Ketchum, M.S. Handbook of standard structural details for buildings. Englewood Cliffs, N.J., Prentice-Hall, 1956.

Kinney, J.S. Indeterminate structural analysis. Reading, Mass., Addison-Wesley, 1957.

Lambe, T.W. Soil testing for engineers. New York, Wiley, 1951.

Large, G.E. Basic reinforced concrete design. 2nd ed. New York, Ronald Press, 1957.

Lin, T.Y. Design of prestressed concrete structures. New York, Wiley, 1955.

Linsley, R.K. and Franzini, J.B. Elements of hydraulic engineering. New York, McGraw-Hill, 1955.

Linsley, R.K. and others. Hydrology for engineers. New York, McGraw-Hill, 1958.

Magill, P.L. and others, eds. Air pollution handbook. New York, McGraw-Hill, 1956.

Peurifoy, R.L. Construction planning, equipment, and methods. New York, McGraw-Hill, 1956.

Rouse, H., ed. Engineering hydraulics; proceedings of the fourth hydraulics conference, Iowa Institute of Hydraulic Research, June 12-15, 1949. New York, Wiley, 1950.

Rudolfs, W., ed. Industrial wastes; their disposal and treatment. New York, Reinhold, 1953.

Seelye, E.E. Foundations: design and practice. New York, Wiley, 1956.

Spangler, M.G. Soil engineering. Scranton, Pa., International Textbook, 1951.

Staley, H.R. Semi-fireproof construction. Princeton, N.J., Van Nostrand, 1948.

Taylor, D.W. Fundamentals of soil mechanics. New York, Wiley, 1948.

Terzaghi, C. and Peck, R.B. Soil mechanics in engineering practice. New York, Wiley, 1948.

Thresh, J.C. The examination of waters and water supplies. 7th ed. by E.W. Taylor. Boston, Little, Brown, 1958.

Urquhart, L.C. and others. Design of concrete structures. 5th ed. New York, McGraw-Hill, 1954.

Wilbur, J.B. and Norris, C.H. Elementary structural analysis. New York, McGraw-Hill, 1948.

Electrical engineering.

Adkins, Bernard. The general theory of electrical machines. London, Chapman & Hall, 1957.

Albert, A.L. Electrical communication. 3rd ed. New York, Wiley, 1950.

Andronov, A.A. and Chaikin, C.E. Theory of oscillations. English language ed., ed. under the direction of Solomon Lefschetz. Princeton, N.J., Princeton Univ. Press, 1949.

Arguimbau, L.B. Vacuum-tube circuits and transistors. With transistor contributions by Richard Brooks Adler. New York, Wiley, 1956.

Beranek, L.L. Acoustics. New York, McGraw-Hill, 1954.

Boast, W.B. Illumination engineering. 2nd ed. New York, McGraw-Hill, 1953.

Bode, H.W. Network analysis and feedback amplifier design. New York, Van Nostrand, 1956(c1945).

Caldwell, S. Switching circuits and logical design. New York Wiley, 1958.

Chestnut, H. and Mayer, R.W. Servomechanisms and regulating system design. New York, Wiley, 1951-55. 2v.

Clarke, E. Circuit analysis of A-C power systems. New York, Wiley, 1943-50. 2v.

Davenport, W.B., Jr. and Root, W.L. Introduction to the theory of random signals and noise. New York, McGraw-Hill, 1958.

Fink, D.G. Television engineering. 2nd ed. New York, McGraw-Hill, 1952.

Fitzgerald, A.E. and Higginbotham, D.E. Basic electrical engineering; circuits, machines, electronics, control. 2nd ed. New York, McGraw-Hill, 1957.

Fitzgerald, A.E. and Kingsley, C. Electric machinery; an integrated treatment of A-C and D-C machines. New York, McGraw-Hill, 1952.

Gardner, M.F. and Barnes, J.L. Transients in linear systems studied by the Laplace transformation. New York, Wiley, 1953(c1942).

Geyger, W.A. Magnetic-amplifier circuits: basic principles. characteristics and applications. 2nd ed. New York, McGraw-Hill, 1957.

Goldman, S. Frequency analysis, modulation and noise. New York, McGraw-Hill, 1948.

Grabbe, E.M. and others, eds. Handbook of automation, computation and control. Vol. 1. New York, Wiley, 1958.

Gray, T.S. Applied electronics: a first course in electronics, electron tubes, and associated circuits. 2nd ed. New York, Wiley, 1954.

Guillemin, E.A. Introductory circuit theory. New York, Wiley, 1953.

Hannay, N.B. Semiconductors. New York, Reinhold, 1959.

Harrington, R.F. Introduction to electromagnetic engineering. New York, McGraw-Hill, 1958.

Harris, F.K. Electrical measurements. New York, Wiley, 1952.

Henney, K. and Richardson, G.A. Principles of radio. 6th ed. New York, Wiley, 1953.

Kerchner, R.M. and Corcoran, G.F. Alternating-current circuits. 3rd ed. New York, Wiley, 1951.

Korn, G.A. and Korn, T.M. Electronic analog computers (d-c analog computers). 2nd ed. New York, McGraw-Hill, 1956.

Reintjes, J.F. and Coate, G.J. Principles of radar. 3rd ed. New York, Technology Press and McGraw-Hill, 1952.

Rider, J.F. and Uslan, S.D. Encyclopedia on cathode-ray oscilloscopes and their uses. New York, J.F. Rider Publisher, 1950.

Rogers, W.E. Introduction to electric fields, a vector analysis approach. New York, McGraw-Hill, 1954.

Roters, H.C. Electromagnetic devices. New York, Wiley, 1941.

Ryder, J.D. Electronic fundamentals and applications. 2nd ed. Englewood Cliffs, N.J., 1959.

Schelkunoff, S.A. Advanced antenna theory. New York, Wiley, 1952.

Schelkunoff, S.A. and Friis, H.T. Antennas: theory and practice. New York, Wiley, 1952.

Skilling, H.H. Transient electric currents. 2nd ed. New York, McGraw-Hill, 1952.

Spangenberg, K.R. Fundamentals of electron devices. New York, McGraw-Hill, 1957.

Terman, F.E. and others. Electronic and radio engineering. 4th ed. New York, McGraw-Hill, 1955.

Van der Ziel, A. Noise. New York, Prentice-Hall, 1954.

White, D.C. and Woodson, H.H. Electro-mechanical energy conversion. New York, Wiley, 1959.

Wiener, N. Cybernetics; or, Control and communication in the animal and the machine. Cambridge, Mass., Technology Press and Wiley, 1948.

Wilkes, M.V. Automatic digital computers. New York, Wiley, 1956.

Zaborsky, J. and Rittenhouse, J.W. Electric power transmission; the power system in the steady state. New York, Ronald Press, 1954.

Zimmerman, H.J. and Mason, S.J. Electronic circuit theory; devices, models, and circuits. New York, Wiley, 1959.

Zworykin, V.K. and Ramberg, E.G. Photoelectricity and its application. New York, Wiley, 1949.

Geology and geophysics.

Barth, T.F.W. Theoretical petrology; a textbook on the origin and the evolution of rocks. New York, Wiley, 1952.

Bateman, A.M. Economic mineral deposits. 2nd ed. New York, Wiley, 1950.

Billings, M.P. Structural geology. 2nd ed. New York, Prentice-Hall, 1954.

Cotton, C.A. Geomorphology. 6th ed. New York, Wiley, 1952.

Dana, J.D. and Hurlbut, C.S. Manual of mineralogy. 17th ed. New York, Wiley, 1959.

Emmons, W.H. and others. Geology; principles and processes. 4th ed. New York, McGraw-Hill, 1955.

Howell, B.F. Introduction to geophysics. New York, McGraw-Hill, 1959.

Jeffreys, H. The earth, its origin, history, and physical constitution. 4th ed. New York, Cambridge [Eng.] University Press, 1959.

Kraus, E.H. and others. Mineralogy. 5th ed. New York, McGraw-Hill, 1959.

Krumbein, W.C. and Sloss, L.L. Stratigraphy and sedimentation. San Francisco, Calif., Freeman, 1951.

Kuenen, P.H. Marine geology. New York, Wiley, 1950.

Leet, L.D. and Judson, S. Physical geology. 2nd ed. New York, Prentice-Hall, 1958.

Levorsen, A.I. Geology of petroleum. San Francisco, Calif., W.H. Freeman, 1954.

Lindgren, W. Mineral deposits. 4th ed. New York, McGraw-Hill, 1933.

Malone, T.F., ed. Compendium of meteorology. Boston, Mass., American Meteorological Society, 1951.

Mather, K.F. Source book in geology. New York, McGraw-Hill, 1939.

Moore, R.C. Introduction to historical geology. 2nd ed. New York, McGraw-Hill, 1958.

Rankama, K. and Sahama, T.G. Geochemistry. Chicago, Ill., Univ. of Chicago, 1950.

Shrock, R.R. and Twenhofel, W.H. Principles of invertebrate paleontology. 2nd ed. New York, McGraw-Hill, 1953.

Sverdrup, H.U. and others. The oceans: their physics, chemistry, and general biology. New York, Prentice-Hall, 1942.

Swinnerton, H.H. Outlines of paleontology. 3rd ed. New York, St. Martin's Press, 1947.

Taylor, G.F. Elementary meteorology. New York, Prentice-Hall 1954.

Trefethen, J.M. Geology for engineers. Princeton, N.J., Van Nostrand, 1949.

Willett, H.C. Descriptive meteorology. 2nd ed. New York, Academic Press, 1957.

Mathematics.

Ahlfors, L.V. Complex analysis; an introduction to the theory of analytic functions of one complex variable. New York, McGraw-Hill, 1953.

Albert, A.A. College algebra. New York, McGraw-Hill, 1946.

Albert, A.A. Fundamental concepts of higher algebra. Chicago, Ill., Univ. of Chicago Press, 1956.

Arnold, J.N. The slide rule; principles and applications. New York, Prentice-Hall, 1954.

Birkoff, G. and MacLane, S. A survey of modern algebra. Rev. ed. New York, Macmillan, 1953.

Churchill, R.V. Operational mathematics. 2nd ed. New York, McGraw-Hill, 1958.

Courant, R. and Robbins, H. What is mathematics? An elementary approach to ideas and methods. New York, Oxford Univ. Press, 1951.

Cramér, H. Elements of probability theory. New York, Wiley, 1955.

Dixon, W.J. and Massey, F.J., Jr. Introduction to statistical analysis. 2nd ed. New York, McGraw-Hill, 1957.

Douglass, R. and Adams, D. Elements of nomography. New York, McGraw-Hill, 1947.

Feller, W. An introduction to probability theory and its applications. Vol. 1. 2nd ed. New York, Wiley, 1957.

Fisher, R.A. The design of experiments. 6th ed. Edinburgh, Oliver and Boyd, 1951.

Fisher, R.A. Statistical methods for research workers. 12th ed., rev. Edinburgh, Oliver and Boyd, 1954.

Fry, T.C. Probability and its engineering uses. New York, Van Nostrand, 1928.

Griffin, H. Elementary theory of numbers. New York, McGraw-Hill, 1954.

Hall, D.W. and Spencer, G.L. Elementary topology. New York, Wiley, 1955.

Halmos, P.R. Finite dimensional vector spaces. 2nd ed. Princeton, N.J., Van Nostrand, 1958.

Halmos, P.R. Measure theory. New York, Van Nostrand, 1950.

Hardy, G.H. A course of pure mathematics. 10th ed. Cambridge [Eng.] University Press, 1952.

Hildebrand, F.B. Advanced calculus for engineers. Ne
Prentice-Hall, 1953.

Hildebrand, F.B. Introduction to numerical analysis. N
McGraw-Hill, 1956.

Hildebrand, F.B. Methods of applied mathematics. Ne
Prentice-Hall, 1952.

Hoel, P.G. Introduction to mathematical statistics. 2nc
New York, Wiley [1958 c1954].

Kells, L.M: Elementary differential equations. 4th ed.
York, McGraw-Hill, 1954.

Kemeny, J.G. and others. Introduction to finite mathematics. Englewood Cliffs, N.J., Prentice-Hall, 1957.

Kendall, M.G. The advanced theory of statistics. London, Griffin, 1952, 1951. 2v. (v. 1, 5th ed.; v. 2, 3rd ed.)

Kershner, R.B. and Wilcox, L.R. Anatomy of mathematics. New York, Ronald Press, 1950.

Kolmogorov, A.N. Foundations of the theory of probability. Transl. by N. Morrison. New York, Chelsea Publ. Co., 1950.

Landau, E.G.H. Foundations of analysis; the arithmetic of whole, rational, irrational and complex numbers. Transl. by F. Steinhardt. New York, Chelsea Publ. Co., 1957(c1951).

Lighthill, M.J. Introduction to Fourier analysis and generalized functions. Cambridge [Eng.] University Press, 1958.

McKinsey, J.C.C. Introduction to the theory of games. New York, McGraw-Hill, 1952.

MacRobert, T.M. Functions of a complex variable. 4th ed. New York, St. Martin's Press, 1954.

Margenau, H. and Murphy, G. M. The mathematics of physics and chemistry. 2nd ed. Princeton, N. J., Van Nostrand, 1956.

Martin, W. T. and Reissner, E. Elementary differential equations. Reading, Mass., Addison-Wesley, 1956.

Miller, K. S. Elements of modern abstract algebra. New York, Harper, 1958.

Milne, W.E. Numerical solution of differential equations. New York, Wiley, 1953.

Morse, P.M. and Kimball, G.E. Methods of operations research. Cambridge, Mass., Technology Press and Wiley, 1951.

Neumann, J. von and Morgenstern, O. Theory of games and economic behavior. 2nd ed. Princeton, N.J., Princeton Univ. Press, 1947.

Pipes, L.A. Applied mathematics for engineers and physicists. 2nd ed. New York, McGraw-Hill, 1958.

Polya, G. How to solve it; a new aspect of mathematical method. Princeton, N.J., Princeton Univ. Press, 1954.

Richards, R.K. Arithmetic operations in digital computers. New York, Van Nostrand, 1955.

Rudin, W. Principles of mathematical analysis. New York, McGraw-Hill, 1953.

Rule, J.T. and Watts, E.F. Engineering graphics. New York, McGraw-Hill, 1951.

Scarborough, J.B. Numerical mathematical analysis. 3rd ed. Baltimore, Md., Johns Hopkins Press, 1955.

Shannon, C.E. and Weaver, W. The mathematical theory of communication. Urbana, Ill., Univ. of Illinois Press, 1949.

Smith, D.E. A source book in mathematics. Cambridge, Mass., Harvard Univ. Press, 1956.

Sneddon, I.N. Fourier transforms. New York, McGraw-Hill, 1951.

Sokolnikoff, I.S. Tensor analysis. New York, Wiley, 1951.

Struik, D.J. Concise history of mathematics. 2nd ed. rev. New York, Dover, 1948.

Struik, D.J. Differential geometry in the large. Reading, Mass., Addison-Wesley, 1950.

Suppes, P. Introduction to logic. Princeton, N.J., Van Nostrand, 1957.

Thomas, G.B., Jr. Calculus and analytic geometry. 2nd ed. Reading, Mass., Addison-Wesley, 1953.

Titchmarsh, E.C. Theory of functions. 2nd ed. New York, Oxford Univ. Press, 1939.

Uspensensky, J.V. Introduction to mathematical probability. New York, McGraw-Hill, 1937.

Vajda, S. Theory of games and linear programming. New York, Wiley, 1956.

Wald, A. Sequential analysis. New York, Wiley, 1947.

Watts, E.F. and Rule, J.T. Descriptive geometry. New York, Prentice-Hall, 1946.

Whittaker, E.T. and Watson, G.N. A course of modern analysis. 4th ed. London, Cambridge [Eng.] University Press, 1927.

Wiener, N. Extrapolation, interpolation and smoothing of stationary time series. New York, Technology Press and Wiley, 1950.

Wiener, N. Fourier integral and certain of its applications. New York, Dover [1951].

Yule, G.U. and Kendall, M.G. An introduction to the theory of statistics. 14th ed. New York, Hafner, 1950.

Mechanical engineering.

Considine, D.M., ed. Process instruments and controls handbook. New York, McGraw-Hill, 1957.

Doughtie, V.L. and James, W.H. Elements of mechanism. New York, Wiley, 1954.

Faires, V.M. Design of machine elements. 3rd ed. New York, Macmillan, 1955.

Faires, V.M. Elementary thermodynamics. 3rd ed. New York, Macmillan, 1957.

Gaffert, G.A. Steam power stations. 4th ed. New York, McGraw-Hill, 1952.

Giesecke, F.E. and others. Technical drawing. 4th ed., rev. by H.C. Spencer. New York, Macmillan, 1958.

Ham, C.W. and others. Mechanics of machinery. 4th ed. New York, McGraw-Hill, 1958.

Hoelscher, R.P. and Springer, C.H. Engineering drawing and geometry. New York, Wiley, 1956.

Jakob, M. and Hawkins, G.A. Elements of heat transfer. 3rd ed. New York, Wiley, 1957.

Jakob, M. Heat transfer. New York, Wiley, 1950-57. 2v.

Jordan, R.C. and Priester, G.B. Refrigeration and air conditioning. 2nd ed. Englewood Cliffs, N.J., 1957.

Judge, A.W. High speed diesel engines...; an elementary textbook for engineers, designers and students. 5th ed. Princeton, N.J., Van Nostrand, 1957.

Keenan, J.H. Thermodynamics. New York, Wiley, 1941.

Kiefer, P.J. and others. Principles of engineering thermodynamics. 2nd ed. New York, Wiley, 1954.

Lewis, B., ed. and others. Combustion processes. Princeton, N.J., Princeton Univ. Press, 1956.

Rogowski, A.R. Elements of internal combustion engines. New York, McGraw-Hill, 1953.

Salisbury, J.K. Steam turbines and their cycles. New York, Wiley, 1950.

Severns, W.H. and Fellows, J.R. Heating, ventilating and air conditioning fundamentals. 2nd ed. New York, Wiley, 1949.

Shepherd, D.G. Principles of turbomachinery. New York, Macmillan, 1956.

Shoop, C.F. and Tuve, G.L. Mechanical engineering practice; a laboratory reference text. 4th ed. New York, McGraw-Hill, 1949.

Taylor, C.F. and Taylor, E.S. The internal combustion engine. Rev. ed. Scranton, Pa., International Textbook, 1948.

Mechanics; Strength of materials.

Chambers, S.D. and Faires, V.M. Analytic mechanics. 3rd ed. New York, Macmillan, 1952.

Crandall, S.H. and Dahl, N.C., eds. An introduction to the mechanics of solids. New York, McGraw-Hill, 1957.

Davis, H.E. and others. The testing and inspection of engineering materials. 2nd ed. New York, McGraw-Hill, 1955.

Den Hartog, J.P. Advanced strength of materials. New York, McGraw-Hill, 1956.

Frocht, M.M. Photoelasticity. New York, Wiley, 1941-48. 2v.

Goodier, J.N. and Hodge, P.G., Jr. Elasticity and plasticity. New York, Wiley, 1958.

Hoffman, O. and Sachs, G. Introduction to the theory of plasticity for engineers. New York, McGraw-Hill, 1953.

Hunsaker, J.C. and Rightmire, B.G. Engineering applications of fluid mechanics. New York, McGraw-Hill, 1947.

Laurson, P.G. and Cox, W.J. Mechanics of materials. 3rd ed. New York, Wiley, 1954.

McCuskey, S.W. An introduction to advanced dynamics. Reading, Mass., Addison-Wesley, 1959.

Marin, J. Engineering materials; their mechanical properties and applications. New York, Prentice-Hall, 1952.

Meriam, J.L. Mechanics. 2nd ed. New York, Wiley, 1959. 2v.

Murray, W. MacG. and Stein, P.K. Strain gage techniques. Cambridge, Massachusetts Institute of Technology, 1957. 2v.

Perry, C.C. and Lissner, H.R. The strain gage primer. New York, McGraw-Hill, 1955.

Prandtl, L. Fundamentals of hydro- and aeromechanics; based on lectures of L. Prandtl, by O. G. Tietjens; transl. by L. Rosenhead. New York, Dover, c1934, 1957.

Shapiro, A.H. Dynamics and thermodynamics of compressible fluid flow. Vol. 1. New York, Ronald Press, 1953.

Rouse, H., ed. Advanced mechanics of fluids. New York, Wiley, 1959.

Rouse, H. and Howe, J.W. Basic mechanics of fluids. New York, Wiley, 1953.

Seely, F.B. and Smith, J.O. Resistance of materials. 4th ed. New York, Wiley, 1956.

Streeter, V.L. Fluid dynamics. New York, McGraw-Hill, 1948.

Streeter, V.L. Fluid mechanics. 2nd ed. New York, McGraw-Hill, 1958.

Synge, J.L. and Griffith, B.A. Principles of mechanics. 2nd ed. New York, McGraw-Hill, 1949.

Timoshenko, S. and Young, D.H. Engineering mechanics. 4th ed. New York, McGraw-Hill, 1956.

Timoshenko, S. Strength of materials. 3rd ed. Princeton, N.J., Van Nostrand, 1955-56. 2v.

Timoshenko, S. Theory of elastic stability. New York, McGraw-Hill, 1936.

Timoshenko, S. and Goodier, J.N. Theory of elasticity. 2nd ed. New York, McGraw-Hill, 1951.

Van Vlack, L.H. Elements of materials science; an introductory text for engineering students. Reading, Mass., Addison-Wesley, 1959.

Wang, C.T. Applied elasticity. New York, McGraw-Hill, 1953.

Mining and metallurgy.

American Institute of Mining and Metallurgical Engineers. Basic open hearth steelmaking. 2nd ed. New York, The Institute, 1951.

Barrett, C.S. Structure of metals; crystallographic methods, principles and data. 2nd ed. New York, McGraw-Hill, 1952.

textbooks and treatises

Bray, J.L. Ferrous process metallurgy. New York, Wiley, 1954.

Darken, L.S. and Gurry, R.W. Physical chemistry of metals. New York, McGraw-Hill, 1953.

Dennis, W.H. Metallurgy of the non-ferrous metals. London, Pitman, 1954.

Dobrin, M.B. Introduction to geophysical prospecting. New York, McGraw-Hill, 1952.

Eve, A.S. and Keys, D.A. Applied geophysics in the search for minerals. 4th ed. Cambridge [Eng.] University Press, 1954.

Gaudin, A.M. Flotation. 2nd ed. New York, McGraw-Hill, 1957.

Gray, A.G., ed. Modern electroplating. New York, Wiley, 1953.

Grossmann, M.A. Principles of heat treatment. Rev. ed. Cleveland, Ohio, American Society for Metals, 1953.

Guy, A.G. Elements of physical metallurgy. 2nd ed. Reading, Mass., Addison-Wesley, 1959.

Hayward, C.R. Outline of metallurgical practice. 3rd ed. Princeton, N.J., Van Nostrand, 1952.

Heine, R.W. and Rosenthal, P.C. Principles of metal casting. New York, McGraw-Hill, 1955.

Kehl, G.L. Principles of metallographic laboratory practice. New York, McGraw-Hill, 1949.

Lewis, R.S. Elements of mining. 2nd ed. New York, Wiley, 1941.

Liddell, D.M. Handbook of non-ferrous metallurgy. 2nd ed. New York, McGraw-Hill, 1945. 2v.

Mott, N.F. and Jones, H. The theory of the properties of metals and alloys. New York, Dover, 1958.

Samans, C.H. Engineering metals and their alloys. New York, Macmillan, 1952.

Schuhmann, R. Metallurgical engineering. Reading, Mass., Addison-Wesley, 1952.

Stoces, B. Introduction to mining. London, Pergamon, 1959. 2v.

Taggart, A.F. Handbook of mineral dressing, ores and industrial minerals. New York, Wiley, 1945.

U.S. Bureau of Mines. Metal mining practice. By C.F. Jackson and J.H. Hedges. (Bulletin 419) Washington, Gov't. Printing Office, 1939.

United States Steel Company. The making, shaping and treating of steel. 7th ed. Pittsburgh, United States Steel Co., 1957.

Wulff, J. and others. Metallurgy for engineers; casting, welding and working. New York, Wiley, 1952.

Young, G.J. Elements of mining. 4th ed. New York, McGraw-Hill, 1946.

Young, J.F. Materials and processes. 2nd ed. New York, Wiley, 1954.

Nuclear engineering.

Benedict, M. and Pigford, T. Nuclear chemical engineering. New York, McGraw-Hill, 1957.

Bonilla, C.F., ed. Nuclear engineering [by] T. Baumeister [and others]. New York, McGraw-Hill, 1957.

Stevenson, R. Introduction to nuclear engineering. 2nd ed. New York, McGraw-Hill, 1958.

Physics.

Abraham, M. The classical theory of electricity and magnetism; rev. by Richard Becker; authorized transl. (based on 14th German ed.) by John Dougall. 2nd ed. New York, Hafner, 1951.

D'Abro, A. The rise of the new physics; its mathematical and physical theories. New York, Dover, 1951. 2v.

Bethe, H.A. and Morrison, P. Elementary nuclear theory. 2nd ed. New York, Wiley, 1956.

Bitter, F. Currents, fields, and particles. New York, Technology Press and Wiley, 1956.

Blatt, J.M. and Weisskopf, V.F. Theoretical nuclear physics. New York, Wiley, 1952.

Bohm, D. Quantum theory. Englewood Cliffs, N.J., Prentice-Hall, 1958(c1951).

Born, Max. Atomic physics. 6th ed. London, Blackie & Son, 1957.

Bozorth, R.M. Ferromagnetism. New York, Van Nostrand, 1951.

Bridgman, P.W. Dimensional analysis. New Haven, Conn., Yale Univ. Press, 1922.

Carslaw, H.S. and Jaeger, J.C. Conduction of heat in solids. 2nd ed. Oxford, Clarendon Press, 1959.

Cohen, E.R. and others. Fundamental constants of physics. New York, Interscience, 1957.

Compton, A.H. and Allison S.K. X-rays in theory and experiment. 2nd ed. Princeton, N.J., Van Nostrand, 1935.

Cork, J.M. Radioactivity and nuclear physics. 3rd ed. Princeton, N.J., Van Nostrand, 1957.

Cowling, T.G. Magnetohydrodynamics. New York, Interscience, 1957.

Crowther, J.A. A manual of physics. 5th ed. New York, Oxford Univ. Press, 1950.

Curtiss, L.F. Introduction to neutron physics. Princeton, N.J., Van Nostrand, 1959.

Dekker, A.J. Solid state physics. Englewood Cliffs, N.J., Prentice-Hall, 1957.

Einstein, A. and Infeld, L. The evolution of physics, the growth of ideas from early concepts of relativity and quanta. New York, Simon and Schuster, 1938.

Einstein, A. The meaning of relativity. 5th ed. Princeton, N.J., Princeton Univ. Press, 1955.

Eisenbud, L. and Wigner, E.P. Nuclear structure. Princeton, N.J., Princeton Univ. Press, 1958.

Evans, R.D. The atomic nucleus. New York, McGraw-Hill, 1955.

Fano, U. and Fano, L. Basic physics of molecules and atoms. New York, Wiley, 1959.

Faraday, M. Experimental researches in electricity. New York, Dutton, 1931.

Frank, N.H. Introduction to electricity and optics. 2nd ed. New York, McGraw-Hill, 1950.

Frank, N.H. Introduction to mechanics and heat. 2nd ed. New York, McGraw-Hill, 1939.

Gibbs, J.W. Collected works. New Haven, Conn., Yale Univ. Press, 1948. 2v.

Glasstone, S. Sourcebook on atomic energy. 2nd ed. New York, Van Nostrand, 1958.

Goldstein, H. Classical mechanics. Reading, Mass., Addison-Wesley, 1953.

Gurney, R.W. Introduction to statistical mechanics. New York, McGraw-Hill, 1949.

Halliday, D. Introductory nuclear physics. 2nd ed. New York, Wiley, 1955.

Hardy, A.C. and Perrin, F.H. Principles of optics. New York, McGraw-Hill, 1932.

Harnwell, G.P. and Livingood, J.J. Experimental atomic physics. 2nd ed. New York, McGraw-Hill, 1933.

Harrison, G.R. and others. Practical spectroscopy. New York, Prentice-Hall, 1948.

Heaviside, O. Electromagnetic theory. New York, Dover, 1950.

Heitler, W. Elementary wave mechanics, with applications to quantum chemistry. 2nd ed. Oxford, Clarendon Press, 1956.

Heitler, W. Quantum theory of radiation. 3rd ed. Oxford, Clarendon Press, 1954.

Herzberg, G. Atomic spectra and atomic structure. 2nd ed. New York, Dover [1944].

Hughes, D.J. Neutron cross sections. London, New York, Pergamon, 1957.

Ingard, U. and Kraushaar, W.L. Interactions and motion. Reading, Mass., Addison-Wesley, 1957-58. 2v.

Jeans, J.H. Mathematical theory of electricity and magnetism. 5th ed. Cambridge [Eng.], The University Press, 1925.

Jeffreys, H. and Jeffreys, B.S. Methods of mathematical physics. 3rd ed. Cambridge [Eng.] University Press, 1956.

Joos, G. Theoretical physics. With the collaboration of I.M. Freeman. 3rd ed. New York, Hafner, 1958.

Kennard, E.H. Kinetic theory of gases, with an introduction to statistical mechanics. New York, McGraw-Hill, 1938.

Kittel, C. Elementary statistical physics. New York, Wiley, 1958.

Lamb, H. Dynamics. 2nd ed. Cambridge [Eng.], The University Press, 1923.

Lamb, Sir H. Hydrodynamics. 6th ed. New York, Dover, 1945.

Landau, L.D. and Lifshitz, E. The classical theory of fields. Transl. by M. Hamermesh. Cambridge, Mass., Addison-Wesley, 1951.

Lemon, H.B. From Galileo to the nuclear age. Rev. ed. Chicago, Ill., Univ. of Chicago Press, 1946.

Lindsay, R.B. Physical mechanics. 2nd ed. New York, Van Nostrand, 1950.

Loeb, L.B. Kinetic theory of gases. 2nd ed. New York, McGraw-Hill, 1934.

Lorentz, H.A. Theory of electrons and its applications to the phenomena of light and radiant heat. 2nd ed. New York, Dover, 1952.

McLachlan, D. X-ray crystal structure. New York, McGraw-Hill, 1957.

Magie, W.F. Source book in physics. New York, McGraw-Hill, 1935.

Massey, H.S.W. and Burhop, E.H.S. Electronic and ionic impact phenomena. Oxford, Clarendon Press, 1952.

Maxwell, J.C. Treatise on electricity and magnetism. Oxford, Clarendon Press, 1873. 2v.

Meyer, C.F. Diffraction of light, X-rays and material particles; an introductory treatment. Chicago, Ill., Univ. of Chicago Press, 1934.

Millikan, R.A. Electrons (+ and -), protons, neutrons, mesotrons and cosmic rays. 2nd ed. Chicago, Ill., Univ. of Chicago, 1947.

Morse, P.M. and Feshbach, H. Methods of theoretical physics. New York, McGraw-Hill, 1953. 2v.

Morse, P.M. Vibration and sound. 2nd ed. New York, McGraw-Hill, 1948.

Mott, N.F. Elements of wave mechanics. Cambridge [Eng.] University Press, 1952.

Mott, N.F. and Massey, H.S.W. Theory of atomic collisions. 2nd ed. Oxford, Clarendon Press [1952].

Page, L. Introduction to theoretical physics. 3rd ed. Princeton, N.J., Van Nostrand, 1952.

Panofsky, W.K.H. and Phillips, M. Classical electricity and magnetism. Reading, Mass., Addison-Wesley, 1955.

Peierls, R.E. The laws of nature. London, Allen & Unwin, 1955.

Peierls, R.E. Quantum theory of solids. Oxford, Clarendon Press, 1955.

Progress in nuclear physics. Vol. 6. London, Pergamon, 1957.

Randall, R.H. An introduction to acoustics. Reading, Mass., Addison-Wesley, 1951.

Rayleigh, J.W.S. Theory of sound; with a historical introduction by R.B. Lindsay. 2nd rev. ed. New York, Dover, 1945. 2v.

Richardson, E.G. Sound; a physical text-book. 5th ed. London, Arnold, 1953.

Richtmyer, F. and Kennard, E.H. Introduction to modern physics. 5th ed. New York, McGraw-Hill, 1955.

Rojansky, V.R. Introductory quantum mechanics. New York, Prentice-Hall, 1950.

Rossi, B.B. High energy particles. New York, Prentice-Hall, 1952.

Rossi, B.B. Optics. Reading, Mass., Addison-Wesley, 1957.

Rossini, F.D., ed. Thermodynamics and physics of matter. Princeton, N.J., Princeton Univ. Press, 1955.

Rushbrooke, G.S. Introduction to statistical mechanics. Oxford, Clarendon Press, 1957(c1949).

Schiff, L.I. Quantum mechanics. 2nd ed. New York, McGraw-Hill, 1955.

Sears, F.W. Mechanics, wave motion and heat. Reading, Mass., Addison-Wesley, 1958.

Sears, F.W. and Zemansky, M.W. University physics. 2nd ed. Reading, Mass., Addison-Wesley, 1955.

Segrè, E. Experimental nuclear physics. New York, Wiley, 1953-1959. 3v.

Seitz, F. Modern theory of solids. New York, McGraw-Hill, 1940.

Sinnott, M.J. The solid state for engineers. New York, Wiley, 1958.

Slater, J.C. and Frank, N.H. Electromagnetism. New York, McGraw-Hill, 1947.

Slater, J.C. and Frank, N.H. Mechanics. New York, McGraw-Hill, 1947.

Slater, J.C. Modern physics. New York, McGraw-Hill, 1955.

Smythe, W.R. Static and dynamic electricity. 2nd ed. New York, McGraw-Hill, 1950.

Sproull, R.L. Modern physics; a textbook for engineers. New York. Wiley. 1956.

Stratton, J.A. Electromagnetic theory. New York, McGraw-Hill, 1941.

Strong, J. and others. Procedures in experimental physics. Englewood Cliffs, N.J., Prentice-Hall, 1956(c1938).

White, H.E. Introduction to atomic spectra. New York, McGraw-Hill, 1934.

von Hippel, A. R., ed. Dielectric materials and applications. New York, Technology Press and Wiley, 1954.

von Hippel, A. R. , and others. Dielectrics and waves. New York, Wiley, 1954.

Wood, R.W. Physical optics. 3rd ed. New York, Macmillan, 1946.

Wooster, W.A. Experimental crystal physics. Oxford, Clarendon Press, 1957.

Zemansky, M.W. Heat and thermodynamics. 4th ed. New York, McGraw-Hill, 1957.

History and philosophy of science; Methodology.

D'Abro, A. The evolution of scientific thought from Newton to Einstein. 2nd ed. rev. and enl. New York, Dover, 1950.

Bridgman, P.W. The logic of modern physics. New York, Macmillan, 1927.

Bridgman, P.W. The nature of physical theory. New York, Dover, 1952.

Bronowski, J. The common sense of science. London, Heinemann, 1951.

Bronowski, J. Science and human values. New York, Messner, 1958.

Butterfield, H. The origins of modern science, 1300-1800. New ed. New York, Macmillan, 1957.

Cohen, M.R. and Nagel, E. An introduction to logic and scientific method. New York, Harcourt, Brace, 1934.

Cohen, M.R. and Drabkin, I.E. A source book in Greek science. New York, McGraw-Hill, 1948.

Conant, J.B. On understanding science; an historical approach. New York, New American Library, 1956.

Crombie, A.C. Augustine to Galileo; history of science A.D. 400-1650. Cambridge, Mass., Harvard Univ. Press, 1953.

Dampier, W.C. A history of science and its relations with philosophy and religion. 4th ed. New York, Macmillan, 1949.

Duhem, P. The aim and structure of physical theory. Princeton, N.J., Princeton Univ. Press, 1954.

Eddington, A.S. The nature of the physical world. New York, Macmillan, 1940.

Forbes, R.J. Man the maker; a history of technology and engineering. London, Abelard-Schuman, 1958.

Galilei, G. Dialogue on the great world systems, in the Salusbury transl. Rev., annotated and with an introd. by G. de Santillana. Chicago, Univ. of Chicago, 1953.

Guerlac, H. Science in western civilization. New York, Ronald Press, 1952.

Hadamard, J. The psychology of invention in the mathematical field. New York, Dover, 1954.

Jeans, J.H. The growth of physical science. New York, Macmillan, 1948.

Kirby, R.S. and others. Engineering in history. New York, McGraw-Hill, 1956.

Lewis, C.I. and Langford, C.H. Symbolic logic. New York, Dover, c1932.

Margenau, H. The nature of physical reality; a philosophy of modern physics. New York, McGraw-Hill, 1950.

Mumford, L. Technics and civilization. New York, Harcourt, 1934.

Parsons, W.B. Engineers and engineering in the Renaissance. Baltimore, Md., Williams and Wilkins, 1939.

Pledge, H.T. Science since 1500; a short history of mathematics, chemistry, physics, and biology. New York, Philosophical Library, 1946.

Poincaré, H. Science and hypothesis. New York, Dover, 1952.

Poincaré, H. Science and method. New York, Dover, 1952.

Reichenbach, H. Philosophy of space and time. New York, Dover.

Santillana, G. de, ed. The age of adventure; the Renaissance philosophers, selected, with introd. and interpretive commentary. Boston, Houghton Mifflin, 1957.

Sarton, G. A history of science. Cambridge, Mass., Harvard Univ. Press, 1952-59. 2v.

Sedgwick, W.T. A short history of science. Rev. ed. New York, Macmillan, 1939.

Singer, C.J. Short history of science to the nineteenth century. Oxford, Clarendon Press, 1941.

Taton, R., ed. Histoire générale des sciences. Paris, Presses Universitaires de France, 1957+. 3v. (projected).

Usher, A.P. A history of mechanical inventions. Cambridge, Mass., Harvard Univ. Press, 1954.

Whitehead, A.N. Process and reality, an essay in cosmology. New York, Humanities Press [1955, (c1929).]

Whitehead, A.N. Science and the modern world. New York, New American Library, c1925.

Wightman, W.P.D. The growth of scientific ideas. Edinburgh, Oliver and Boyd, 1950.

Wilson, E.B., Jr. An introduction to scientific research. New York, McGraw-Hill, 1952.

Wolf, A. History of science, technology and philosophy in the 16th and 17th centuries. 2nd ed. London, Allen & Unwin, 1950.

Wolf, A. History of science, technology and philosophy in the 18th century. 2nd ed. London, Allen & Unwin, 1952.

III. JOURNALS

General.

Académie des Sciences. Comptes rendus hebdomodaires des séances. 1835. Weekly. Paris, Gauthier-Villars.

Annals of science; a quarterly review of the history of science since the renaissance. 1936. Quarterly. London, Taylor and Francis, Ltd.

Bulletin of the atomic scientists; a magazine for science and public affairs. 1945. Monthly. Chicago, Ill., Univ. of Chicago Press.

Daedalus: journal of the American Academy of Arts and Sciences. 1846. Quarterly. Boston, The Academy.

The engineer. 1856. Weekly. London, Engineer.

Engineering. 1866. Weekly. London, Engineering.

Franklin Institute. Journal; devoted to science and the mechanic arts. 1826. Monthly. Philadelphia, Franklin Institute of the State of Pennsylvania.

Isis; international review devoted to the history of science and its cultural influences. 1913. Quarterly. Cambridge, Mass., History of Science Society, Harvard Univ.

Journal of engineering education. 1910. Monthly. Lancaster, Pa., American Society for Engineering Education.

National Academy of Sciences. Proceedings. 1915. Monthly. Chicago, Ill., Univ. of Chicago Press.

Nature. 1869. Weekly. London, Macmillan.

Philosophy of science. 1934. Quarterly. Baltimore, Md., Williams and Wilkins.

Science. 1880. Weekly. Washington, American Association for the Advancement of Science.

Science newsletter. 1921. Weekly. Washington, D.C., Science Service.

Scientific American. 1845. Monthly. New York, Scientific American.

Aeronautical engineering.

Aero/space engineering. 1942. Monthly. New York, Institute of the Aeronautical Sciences.

ARS journal. 1930. Monthly. New York, American Rocket Society and American Interplanetary Society.

Aviation week. 1916. Weekly. New York, McGraw-Hill.

Flight, aircraft, spacecraft, missiles. 1910. Weekly. London, Iliffe and Sons.

Interavia; a review of world aviation. 1946? Monthly. Geneva, Switzerland, Interavia S.A.

Journal of the aero/space sciences. 1934. Monthly. New York, Institute of the Aeronautical Sciences.

Missiles and rockets; magazine of world astronautics. 1956. Weekly. Washington, American Aviation Publications.

Royal Aeronautical Society. Journal. 1897. Monthly. London, The Society.

Astronomy.

Astronomical journal. 1849. Irregular (8-12 nos. per year). New Haven, Conn., American Astronomical Society, Yale Univ. Observatory.

Astrophysical journal; an international review of spectroscopy and astronomical physics. 1895. Bi-monthly. Chicago, Ill., Univ. of Chicago Press.

Royal Astronomical Society of London. Monthly notices. 1827. 6 nos. per year. London, The Society.

Sky and telescope. 1941. Monthly. Cambridge, Mass., Sky Publ. Corp.

Biology.

American Institute of Biological Sciences. Bulletin; news and views in the biological sciences. 1951. 5 times per year. Washington, American Institute of Biological Sciences.

American journal of botany; devoted to all branches of plant sciences. 1914. Monthly. East Lansing, Mich., Michigan State College.

American journal of physiology. 1898. Monthly. Washington, American Physiological Society.

American naturalist; devoted to the advancement and correlation of the biological sciences. 1867. Bi-monthly. Lancaster, Pa., Science Press.

Annals of botany. 1878. Quarterly. London, Oxford Univ. Press.

Biochemical journal. 1906. Monthly. London, Biochemical Society.

Biological reviews of the Cambridge philosophical society. 1923. Quarterly. London, Cambridge Univ. Press.

Botanical gazette. 1875. Quarterly. Chicago, Ill., Univ. of Chicago Press.

Evolution; international journal of organic evolution. 1947. Quarterly. Lancaster, Pa., Society for the Study of Evolution.

Journal of biological chemistry. 1905. Monthly. Baltimore, Md., Williams and Wilkins Co.

Journal of experimental zoology. 1904. Monthly. except May, September, January. Philadelphia, Pa., Wistar Institute of Anatomy and Biology.

Journal of heredity. 1910. Bi-monthly. Baltimore, Md., American Genetic Association.

Natural history. 1900. Monthly. New York, American Museum of Natural History.

Physiological reviews. 1921. Quarterly, Washington, American Physiological Society.

Quarterly review of biology. 1926. Quarterly. Baltimore, Md., Published for the American Institute of Biological Sciences by the Williams and Wilkins Co.

Royal Society. Proceedings. Series B: Biological sciences. 1800. Irregular. London, The Society.

Chemical engineering.

A.I.Ch.E. journal. 1955. Quarterly. New York, American Institute of Chemical Engineers.

Chemical and engineering news. 1923. Weekly. Washington, American Chemical Society.

Chemical engineering. 1902. Monthly. New York, McGraw-Hill.

Chemical engineering progress. 1908. Monthly. Philadelphia, Pa., American Institute of Chemical Engineers.

Chemistry and industry. 1923. Weekly. London, Society of Chemical Industry.

Industrial and engineering chemistry. 1909. Monthly. Washington, American Chemical Society.

Journal of applied chemistry. 1951. Monthly. London, Society of Chemical Industry.

Chemistry.

American Chemical Society. Journal. 1879. Semi-monthly. Washington, The Society.

The analyst. 1877. Monthly. Cambridge, England. Society for Analytical Chemistry.

Analytical chemistry. 1929. Monthly. Washington, American Chemical Society.

Chemical reviews. 1924. Bi-monthly. Baltimore, Md., Williams and Wilkins.

Chemical Society. Annual reports on the progress of chemistry. 1904. Annual. London, The Society.

Chemical Society of London. Journal. 1841. Monthly. London, The Society.

Journal of chemical education. 1924. Monthly. New York, American Chemical Society.

Journal of organic chemistry. 1936. Monthly. Baltimore, Md., Williams and Wilkins.

Journal of physical chemistry. 1896. Monthly. Washington, American Chemical Society.

Quarterly reviews. 1947. Quarterly. London, Chemical Society.

Civil and sanitary engineering; Building construction.

American Concrete Institute. Journal and proceedings. 1929. Monthly. Detroit, Mich., The Institute.

American Society of Civil Engineers. Proceedings. 1873. Several papers each month. New York, The Society.

American Water Works Association. Journal. 1914. Monthly. New York, The Association.

Architectural forum. 1892. Monthly. New York, Time Inc.

Architectural record. 1891. Monthly. New York, F.W. Dodge Corp.

Civil engineering. 1930. Monthly. New York, American Society of Civil Engineers.

Engineering news-record. 1874. Weekly. New York, McGraw-Hill.

Public works; city, county and state. 1895. Monthly. Ridgewood, N.J., Public Works Journal Corp.

Sewage and industrial wastes. 1928. Monthly. Washington, Federation of Sewage and Industrial Wastes Associations.

Electrical engineering.

American Institute of Electrical Engineers. Transactions. 1884. Annual in three parts. New York, The Institute.

Bell system technical journal; devoted to the scientific and engineering aspects of electrical communication. 1922. Bi-monthly. New York, American Telephone and Telegraph Co.

Electrical engineering. 1887. Monthly. New York, American Institute of Electrical Engineers.

Electronics. 1930. Weekly. New York, McGraw-Hill.

Institute of Radio Engineers. Proceedings. 1913. Monthly. New York, The Institute.

Institution of Electrical Engineers. Proceedings. 1872. Monthly. London, The Institution.

Geology and geophysics.

American journal of science. 1818. Monthly. New Haven, Conn., Yale Univ. Press.

American Meteorological Society. Bulletin. 1920. Monthly. Lancaster, Pa., The Society.

American mineralogist; journal of the Mineralogical Society of America. 1916. Bi-monthly. Ann Arbor, Mich., American Mineralogist.

Economic geology and the Bulletin of the Society of Economic Geologists. 1905. 8 times per year. Urbana, Ill., Economic Geology Publ. Co.

Geological Society of America. Bulletin. 1889. Monthly. New York, The Society.

Journal of geology. 1893. Bi-monthly. Chicago, Ill., Univ. of Chicago Press.

Journal of geophysical research. 1896. Quarterly. Chicago, Ill., Univ. of Chicago Press.

Journal of paleontology. 1927. Bi-monthly. Tulsa, Okla., Society of Economic Paleontologists and Mineralogists and the Paleontological Society.

U.S. Weather Bureau. Monthly weather review. 1872. Monthly. Washington, Gov't. Printing Office.

Weatherwise. 1948. Bi-monthly. Philadelphia, Pa., American Meteorological Society.

Mathematics.

American journal of mathematics. 1878. 4 times per year. Baltimore, Md., American Mathematical Society, Johns Hopkins Press.

American mathematical monthly. 1894. 10 times per year. Menasha, Wis., Mathematical Association of America.

American Mathematical Society. Bulletin. 1891. Bi-monthly. Providence, R.I., American Mathematical Society.

American Statistical Association. Journal. 1888. Quarterly. Washington, The Association.

Journal of mathematics and physics. 1921. Quarterly. Cambridge, Mass., Massachusetts Inst. of Technology.

Journal of research of the National Bureau of Standards. 1928. Section B. Mathematics and mathematical physics. Quarterly. Washington, Gov't. Printing Office.

Mathematical gazette. 1894. Quarterly. London, Mathematical Association.

Mathematics magazine. 1926. 5 times per year. Pacoima, Calif., Mathematics Magazine.

Mathematics teacher. 1908. Monthly (Oct.-May). Washington, National Council of Teachers of Mathematics.

Quarterly of applied mathematics. 1943. Quarterly. Providence, R.I., Brown Univ.

Mechanical engineering.

Air conditioning, heating, and ventilating. 1906. Monthly. New York, Industrial Press.

Institution of Mechanical Engineers. Journal and Proceedings. 1847. Monthly. London, The Institution.

Journal of applied mechanics; transactions of the ASME, Series E. 1933. Quarterly. Easton, Pa., American Society of Mechanical Engineers.

Journal of basic engineering; transactions of the ASME, Series D. 1959. Quarterly. Easton, Pa., American Society of Mechanical Engineers.

Journal of engineering for industry; transactions of the ASME, Series B. 1959. Quarterly. Easton, Pa., American Society of Mechanical Engineers.

Journal of engineering for power; transactions of the ASME, Series A. 1959. Quarterly. Easton, Pa., American Society of Mechanical Engineers.

Journal of heat transfer; transactions of the ASME, Series C. 1959. Quarterly. Easton, Pa., American Society of Mechanical Engineers.

Machine design. 1929. Bi-monthly. Cleveland, Ohio, Penton Publ. Co.

Mechanical engineering. 1906. Monthly. New York, American Society of Mechanical Engineers.

Product engineering. 1930. Monthly. New York, McGraw-Hill.

S.A.E. journal. 1917. Monthly. New York, Society of Automotive Engineers.

Welding journal. 1922. Monthly. New York, American Welding Society.

Mining and metallurgy.

Engineering and mining journal. 1866. Monthly. New York, McGraw-Hill.

Institute of Metals. Journal. 1909. Monthly. London, Institute of Metals.

Iron and Steel Institute. Journal. 1869. Monthly. London, Iron and Steel Institute.

Journal of metals. 1949. Monthly. New York, American Institute of Mining and Metallurgical Engineers.

Metal progress. 1920. Monthly. Cleveland, Ohio, American Society for Metals.

Mining engineering. 1949. Monthly. New York, American Institute of Mining and Metallurgical Engineers.

Nuclear engineering.

Nuclear science and engineering: the journal of the American Nuclear Society. 1956. Bi-monthly. New York, Academic Press.

Physics.

Acoustical Society of America. Journal. 1929. Monthly. New York, The Society.

Advances in physics; a Quarterly supplement to the Philosophical magazine. 1952. Quarterly. London, Taylor and Francis.

American journal of physics. 1933. Monthly. New York, American Institute of Physics.

Journal of applied physics. 1930. Monthly. New York, American Institute of Physics.

Journal of chemical physics. 1933. Monthly. New York, American Institute of Physics.

Journal of research of the National Bureau of Standards. 1928. Section A. Physics and chemistry. Bi-monthly. Washington, Gov't. Printing Office.

Journal of Scientific Instruments. 1923. Monthly. London, Institute of Physics.

Nucleonics. 1947. Monthly. New York, McGraw-Hill.

Optical Society of America. Journal. 1917. Monthly. New York, American Institute of Physics.

Philosophical magazine; a journal of theoretical, experimental and applied physics. 1798. Monthly. London, Taylor and Francis.

Physical review, 1893. Semi-monthly. New York, American Institute of Physics.

Physical review letters. 1958. Semi-monthly. New York, American Physical Society.

Physical Society. Proceedings. Sections A and B. 1874. Monthly. London, Physical Society.

Physical Society. Reports on progress in physics. 1934. Annual. London, The Society.

Physics today. 1948. Monthly. New York, American Institute of Physics.

Review of scientific instruments. 1930. Monthly. New York, American Institute of Physics.

Reviews of modern physics. 1929. Quarterly. New York, American Institute of Physics.

Royal Society. Proceedings. Ser. A. Mathematical and physical sciences. 1800. Irregular. London, The Society.

www.ingramcontent.com/pod-product-compliance
Lightning Source LLC
Chambersburg PA
CBHW061207180526
45170CB00002B/996

9780262100021